Inconsolable

A Christian Devotional for Heavyhearted Grievers

Julie Jones

In Memory of Kyle Christopher Jones

DEDICATION

Kyle Christopher Jones

To Kyle, my beloved son. Thank you for so many golden memories. Your life was an unrepeatable miracle. You leave behind a place that cannot be filled. I am devastated that you have gone and I miss you desperately. Save me a seat beside you at the banqueting table. We will laugh and celebrate again. Until then, pray for us.

To Eric, my beloved son. You have been a God-given anchor during a horrific storm and have kept me from floating away in the waves of grief. Thank you for standing by me and sharing your strength.

To Alex and Julie, my beloved son and beloved daughter-in-law. You are a perpetual source of encouragement and comfort. Thank you for being radiant beacons of hope for the future.

To Jerry, my beloved husband and Kyle's earthly father. You alone share the depth of my love for Kyle and the depth of my despair. You alone will share the depth of my joy when we hold our son again. What a day of rejoicing that will be!

To all of you listed above who I love so much, and to all future generations of our family - I pray you will live a life of love and leave a legacy of faith. Trust in the Lord and His unfailing love.

"Your name, Lord, endures forever, your renown, Lord, through all generations (of our family.)" Psalm 135:13

Heartfelt thanks and gratitude to Eric for designing this book's cover, and to my proof readers: Amy, Coraly, Julie, Jerry and Alex. You made this a better book.

TO THE READER

I wrote this book over several years after the death of my son and in it I share what grief has been like for me. This is a Christian devotional based on scriptures from the NIV Bible. It is intended to be read over seven weeks, one devotion each day.

My aim is to help people who are bereaved and have heavy hearts to do the things I am learning to do – grieve with hope, forgive, think of Heaven, rely on God, invest in eternity, persevere, and have confident faith.

In this book I talk about the assurance I have of my son's salvation because I know he put his trust in Jesus. If your loved one has died and you do not have the assurance of knowing they believed in Jesus, I encourage you to be hopeful. Faith is a gift from God and He may have given your loved one that gift at any time without your knowledge of it.

I am so sorry for your loss and your grief. Life has changed for you and I. We cannot expect the wound of our loss to completely heal or life to ever be the same again because someone significant will always be missing. As C.S. Lewis wrote, "The death of a beloved is an amputation."

May God have mercy on all of us heavyhearted grievers.

"For in grief nothing stays put. One keeps on emerging from a phase, but it always recurs. Round and round. Everything repeats. Am I going in circles, or dare I hope I am on a spiral? But if on a spiral, am I going up or down it? How often – will it be for always? – how often will the vast emptiness astonish me like a complete novelty and make me say, "I never realized my loss till this moment?" The same leg is cut off time after time." C.S. Lewis, A Grief Observed

CONTENTS

INTRODUCTION

There is an ancient memorial stone in the floor of the church at the San Juan Bautista Mission in California. The stone is engraved with a young man's name, his birth and death dates in the 1800's, and the Spanish words "Su familia inconsolable." I stand over the cobbled stone and slowly nod my head as grief wells up and spills from my eyes. I know this family's pain. To lose a son and a brother is devastating. I know because it happened to my family too. We are bereaved. We are broken. We are inconsolable. We are like Rachel weeping for her children and refusing to be comforted. (Jeremiah 31:15)

You can go through your whole life fixing every broken thing – broken relationships, broken bones, broken promises. You can get through tough times by working hard and believing better days are ahead. You can handle all life brings your way – until you can't. Until life gives you something you cannot fix no matter how hard you work or how strongly you believe. In one unexpected moment something can be taken from you that you cannot live without and you cannot get back. You can become inconsolable.

I think back to the time I brought my son, Kyle to visit this historical California Mission. He was 10 years old and he and I were completing an independent study of California History. We browsed the gift shop and he chose a metal coin-like medallion engraved with the words, *"Have faith in God for in times of trouble He will carry you."* He kept that medallion in his pocket for many years along with his other little-boy treasures. I found it in the clothes dryer many times. I found it in his apartment the day after he died.

On this day, I go to the gift shop and buy a candle. I set it on a side alter and light it. I get on my knees before God on the wooden kneeler and I pray. I'm not Catholic, and I don't know what I'm doing, but I'm hoping to get God's attention. I am like Hagar in the wilderness. (Genesis 16:13) Do You see me God? Do You see me in this wilderness of despair with no hope apart from You?

I think of the little medallion. *"Have faith in God for in times of trouble He will carry you."* Did You carry my son, Lord? Did You carry him away? My heart is broken beyond repair. I'm in the worst kind of trouble. I don't have the strength for this kind of trouble. Will You carry me?

Jesus said, **"Blessed are those who mourn, for they shall be comforted." (Matthew 5:4)**

I don't want to mourn and I don't want comfort. I only want my son!

"Call me Mara, because the Almighty has made my life very bitter." (Ruth 1:20)

My heart is a hard stone engraved with the word "inconsolable."

<u>Week One</u>

GRIEVE WITH HOPE

When a county sheriff came to my home in Missouri on a snowy February morning in 2012 and told me that my son, Kyle had been found dead in his Texas apartment, the only hope I had was that this was a mistake. They had the wrong house, the wrong son, the wrong Mom. Until I saw my son's body, my hope was that this horrible thing was not true.

It took a long time for my heart to believe what my head knew – there was nothing I could do. I wanted to fix this, I wanted to DO something. I didn't want to give up hope that Kyle would be okay and life could go on as expected. The mystery that clouded Kyle's death didn't help. Somehow I thought that if I could just pinpoint what went wrong it could be fixed.

The police detective said it was medical. Kyle had been complaining of stomach aches, but healthy 24-year-olds don't die from stomach aches. The autopsy showed the cause of death to be a gastrointestinal hemorrhage caused by acute inflammation. But what caused the inflammation? There were many possibilities, and as time went on it became clear we would never know for sure.

After telling us all he could, the police detective brought in a grief counselor to talk to us. She told us we would all grieve differently and we shouldn't blame anyone – not ourselves, not each other, and not Kyle.

"24-year-old young men think they are invincible," she said, "they don't take care of themselves and they don't go to doctors." She warned us about what was ahead of us – denial, anger, blame, regret, and depression. "Get ready to walk the hell-road," she warned.

As I write this, I am two years down the "hell road" the police counselor described. It has probably been as close to hell as one can get on earth, but hell is the absence of God, and God has not been absent. He has filled me with great hope of all that is still to come, and has assured me that my son is alive and well in Heaven. Previously my hope was focused on this temporary life that passes so quickly. My hope was in the wrong place. My hope is now in Heaven – a perfect place where life never ends, where loved ones never leave, where dreams never die – where my son LIVES.

Grieve With Hope

"Brothers and sisters, we do not want you to be uninformed about those who sleep in death, so that you do not grieve like the rest of mankind, who have no hope. For we believe that Jesus died and rose again, and so we believe that God will bring with Jesus those who have fallen asleep in Him."
1 Thess. 4:13-14

People have been dying and families have been grieving since Cain killed Abel, but when it happens to someone you love, to your family, it feels like you are the first and only people to lose someone and to feel the awful despair of grief. It can be hard to focus on the hope that we have in Christ when we are hurting so badly and missing our loved one so much.

The word hope as it is used in this scripture means having faith, not wishing or wishful thinking. The apostle Paul wrote the above words to the Thessalonians to remind them that, as Christians, we are not to grieve like the rest of the world. He didn't tell them not to grieve – that would not be possible, desirable, or healthy – he told them to grieve with hope. Because Jesus died and then rose again we can know FOR SURE that our loved ones who died believing in Christ have also been brought back to life. Their spirits are alive in Heaven and when Christ returns their bodies will be resurrected too.

Hope of seeing our loved ones again does not make the pain of missing them any less, but it does help us when we think about our loved ones to think of the joy and peace they have in Heaven and to remember that our separation is only temporary.

It helps me to read all I can about Heaven as it is now, and the new Heaven and new earth that are to come when Jesus returns. The above scripture tells us the way to grieve with hope is to become informed about our loved ones who have gone ahead. There are many good and biblical books written about Heaven and I have listed some of my favorites at the end of this book.

Prayer: Father God, give me the faith to believe in all your promises and to grieve with the hope I and my loved one share in Christ. I have never known such pain and I will not survive unless you help me. Have mercy on me as you teach me what it means to grieve with hope. Amen.

It's Okay to Cry

"Jesus wept." John 11:35

Jesus wept when his friend, Lazarus died. Christians grieve when loved ones die. Death separates us and it hurts. We want our loved ones with us. We want to talk to them, spend time with them, and share our life with them. Death takes them out of our reach. We can no longer communicate with them. We can't tell them we love them or hear them say they love us. We had plans and dreams that will never happen. We were unable to control the circumstances that caused our loved one's death. We are angry, bitter, sad, regretful, vengeful, and our souls are heavy with sorrow. We don't know how we will go on with life without this one we love so much. We weep as Jesus wept because death hurts.

I cried every day for over a year and then, slowly, didn't cry as much anymore. I was heartbroken. I had suffered an unrecoverable loss. (The greater the loss, the greater the grief.) I pleaded with God for this to not be true. I begged God to bring my son back, to turn back the hands of time. "Please God, let me wake up and find out this was only a bad dream."

God cares about our sorrow and weeping. ***Psalm 56:8 says, "You keep track of all my sorrows. You have collected all my tears in your bottle. You have recorded each one in your book."*** Our tears are valuable to God and crying is valuable to us too during this time of immense sorrow. Our tears are a release of the intense emotions we are feeling.

We may grieve deeply and we may grieve long but if we are allowing The Lord to come alongside us in our grief, then we are grieving with hope. Hope that our loved one is not gone, just separated from us for a time. Hope that our loved one is rejoicing and praising God in Heaven. Hope that when this brief life is over, we will be with our loved one again.

Prayer: Father God, thank you for the gift of tears that help me to express my immense sorrow. Be with me as I grieve deeply for as long as it takes. Fill me with all the hope that I have in Christ. Please help me to endure this overwhelming despair. Amen.

Take Your Time

"Now is your time of grief, but I will see you again and you will rejoice, and no one will take away your joy." John 16:22

Grief lasts for a time – for a season. There are no clear parameters for how long your grief will last because every time of grief is unique. Your grief will last as long as it lasts. When it seems like the dark days of depression are dragging on and on, remember this promise from Jesus...we will see Him again and we will rejoice. And we will see our loved ones again too. Then we will rejoice with the security of knowing that our joy will never end. No person or circumstance will be able to take away our joy. Our joy will be eternal.

Remembering back to my son's college days, it was always such a joyous time when he came home during school breaks. The anticipation of his coming home was wonderful. I would purchase the groceries he especially liked, prepare his room, and make his favorite foods. There was just nothing like the moment he arrived and I saw his face and hugged him close. All too soon the visit would end and he would leave to go back to school. I cried every time because it seemed unbearable that I would not see him again for many months.

Now my son has gone to Heaven and I don't know how long it will be before I see him again. Jesus may return or I may be called home any day, or it may be decades before I am reunited with my son. But I know a time is coming when I will see my son and then will never have to say good bye again. We will be together in a perfect place where sorrow and sadness are just not allowed. Nothing can break my heart in Heaven. Heaven is a place of homecomings, feasts, and rejoicing that never ends. (Rev. 19:7-10)

We do not know how long our grief will last, but we do know how long our joy will last. Forever!

Prayer: Father God, I pray You will take away all my expectations about how long I think my grief should last and will give me endurance for all the hard days ahead. Thank you that a day is coming when I will be filled with unending joy. My hope is in you. Amen.

Live by Faith

"Therefore we are always confident and know that as long as we are at home in the body we are away from the Lord. For we live by faith, not by sight. We are confident, I say, and would prefer to be away from the body and at home with the Lord."
2 Corinthians 5:6-8

The apostle Paul, in his letter to the Corinthian church, says we are always confident that our final destination is with the Lord and we will get there when we leave our earthly bodies. Our bodies are perishable and cannot inherit the Kingdom of God. As long as we are clothed in our perishable bodies we will be away from the Lord.

We cannot yet see our destination so we don't know of it by sight, but we know of it by faith. When we get to Heaven we will no longer be living by faith but rather by sight because we will see it with our own eyes.

Paul says we can be so confident that we will reach our destination that if given the choice we would prefer to go there now – to leave our body and be at home with the Lord.

I'm comforted knowing my son has seen the Lord with his own eyes and is now living by sight. I'm challenged as I live by faith because I cannot communicate with my son and my communication with God is often unclear.

I am prone to give in to despair and doubt. I remind myself that the Bible and Jesus' life, death and resurrection are well-documented historical facts. I think about all the times God has made Himself real to me and I have felt His presence. I look at nature and know this amazing planet we live on could not be a random accident. We have a Creator, a Sustainer, a Sovereign Lord. He is all He claims to be and I can trust Him.

By faith, I agree with Paul that it is preferable to be away from the body and at home with the Lord.

Prayer: Christ Jesus, help me to grow in confidence that it is better for my loved one to be with You in Heaven then here on earth with me. I pray you will lead me to the scriptures that will give me the assurance and peace I need as I live by faith. Let each day bring me evidence of Your unfailing love as I put all my hope in You. Amen.

See the Unseen

"Therefore we do not lose heart. Though outwardly we are wasting away, yet inwardly we are being renewed day by day. For our light and momentary troubles are achieving for us an eternal glory that far outweighs them all. So we fix our eyes not on what is seen, but on what is unseen, since what is seen is temporary, but what is unseen is eternal." 2 Corinthians 4:16-18

Don't lose heart – don't despair, don't be discouraged, and don't give up. Don't look at what you can see – look at what is unseen and eternal. Hope in what is seen is hope in the temporary and will lead to despair because what we can see is wasting away. If this life is all there is, we have reason to despair, because it is fleeting and filled with trouble. But this life won't last forever, and in some way, our suffering during this life earns us glory in eternity.

When we lose a loved one we are reminded of the frailty of the human body. As our own bodies deteriorate we have evidence our body is only a temporary home. But we are not to despair because even though our bodies are wasting away on the outside, God is renewing our souls on the inside.

This scripture says our troubles are "light and momentary." My grief feels the opposite. It feels heavy and unending, but that is because I am in the thick of it. Looking back on other seasons of my life, they seem to have passed very quickly.

We may be losing loved ones, we may be losing our health and our youthful abilities, but we are not to lose heart. We cannot stop time or control the changes that come with time, but we can put our faith and trust in the One who is able to do all things. As we waste away on the outside we are being built up on the inside. This is God's promise to us – that our suffering has an eternal purpose.

Prayer: Father God, build me up on the inside even as I am wasting away on the outside. Remind me that all my troubles are temporary and are earning me glory in Heaven. Help me when I am weighed down with sorrow and despair to remember that it won't last forever. Help me to think less about this temporary life and to think more about my eternal life with you and my loved ones in Heaven. Amen.

Remember God's Great Love

"Yet this I call to mind and therefore I have hope: Because of the Lord's great love we are not consumed, for His compassions never fail. They are new every morning; great is your faithfulness." Lamentations 3:21-23

My Bible notes tell me Lamentations 3 was written by a man who endured suffering and yet experienced God's faithfulness. Too often we judge God's character by our circumstances instead of rightly interpreting our circumstances by what we know of God's character.

This verse tells us we have to call to mind the reason for our hope. We can't trust our grief-fogged brains to bring these things to mind, nor our embittered emotions and crushed hearts to feel like thinking good thoughts about God. We must take action by actively recalling all we know about God. We must remind ourselves of His unfailing love, compassion, and faithfulness to us and to our loved ones who are now in Heaven.

I strive to remember God's great love so that I will not be consumed by my grief. I recall God's compassion and know He will not fail me and He has not failed my son.

Each morning is a new day in which anything is possible. I look for God's restoration and redemption. I remember God's great faithfulness and His promise to never leave me nor forsake me. (Deut. 31:6)

The apostle Paul wrote to Timothy of his hope in God's faithfulness from a cold dungeon, *"...I know whom I have believed, and am convinced that he is able to guard what I have entrusted to him until that day." (2 Timothy 1:12)*

Like Paul, I am learning to interpret my circumstances by what I know of God's perfect character rather than judging God's character by my difficult circumstances.

Prayer: *"May our Lord Jesus Christ himself and God our Father, who loved us and by his grace gave us eternal encouragement and good hope, encourage our hearts and strengthen us in every good deed and word." (2 Thessalonians 2:16-17) Amen.*

Put Your Hope in God

"Why, my soul, are you downcast? Why so disturbed within me? Put your hope in God, for I will yet praise Him, my Savior and my God." Psalm 42:5

When you are in the deep throes of depression, when your soul is downcast and disturbed, it's hard to have hope that brighter days are ahead. In this verse the psalmist is talking to his own depressed soul. "Why are you feeling this way?," he asks.

There may be nothing you alone can do to pull yourself out of the pit of despair, but with God everything is possible. (Matt. 19:26) If you can do nothing else, you can always do this one thing – put your hope in God. Put your hope in the Creator and Sustainer of the Universe. Put your hope in the One who raised Christ from the dead. Even if at this time you cannot praise Him, put your hope in the promise that a day is coming when you will again have much for which to praise Him. Remember all that He is to you – your Savior and your God.

I like this idea of talking to my own soul and convincing it to persevere in hope in God. Along with talking to my soul, I also need to remember to talk to God, telling Him how overwhelming my sadness is and how much I need His help to be hopeful.

I often wake up in the morning feeling sad. When I do, I like to pray this verse to God. *"Let this morning bring me word of your unfailing love, for I have put my trust in you. Show me the way I should go, for to you I entrust my life." (Psalm 143:8)*

Asking God to bring me word of His unfailing love gives me the motivation to get out of bed to see what God will do.

After praying this prayer I open my Bible expecting to be encouraged. Later, I might go for a walk and expect to see something in nature that reminds me of God's goodness and power.

I am limited in the things I can do to improve my hope, but God is never limited in what He can do.

Prayer: My Savior, my God, remind me to encourage my own soul with the promise that when I put my hope in You I will always have cause to praise You. Thank You for your promise that those who hope in You will never be put to shame. (Psalm 25:3) Amen.

Week Two

FORGIVE

On the Friday before Kyle died, he became sick at work. Two of his co-workers observed that he was dizzy and slurring his speech. According to what they said, they offered to take him to get medical care but he declined. They offered to drive him home but he again declined saying he would need his car on the weekend. They convinced him to let them drive him home promising to come get him on Saturday and take him to get his car. One of the co-workers dropped him off at home on Friday afternoon. The other co-worker called him on Saturday but he didn't answer his phone or return the call. She called him again on Sunday – again no answer or returned call. When she got to work on Monday and saw that Kyle's car was there but Kyle was absent, she became alarmed and notified the company's human resources department. H.R. contacted Kyle's supervisor who called Kyle, went to his apartment, and eventually called the police. By the time they got into Kyle's apartment he had died, but he had only been dead a few hours. Quicker action on Monday morning or action anytime on Saturday or Sunday would most likely have saved him. A different action on Friday afternoon absolutely would have saved him. We were told by the police detective who had consulted with a physician that Kyle's condition did not need to end in death. If Kyle had been given IV fluids he would not have died.

I was overcome with anger at the stupidity and ineptness of Kyle's co-workers. Why in the world didn't they call paramedics on Friday afternoon? Dizziness and slurred speech are symptoms of many serious medical emergencies. Why didn't they do something when he didn't answer his phone on the weekend? Why did it take hours to get to him on Monday morning? Why did everyone fail to help Kyle? Clearly there were many people who could be held accountable, many people to be angry with, and ultimately, many people to forgive.

Knowing I needed to leave these hurtful people and their careless actions in God's hands isn't the same as doing it. In the early days of my grief I was desperate to pinpoint what went wrong so I could fix it. Yes, it's illogical, but that's where my grief-saturated brain was at.

I wanted my son back and I wanted this horrible thing to be not true. I wanted these people to explain to me why they had made such poor choices with my son's life.

When we or someone we love is hurt, revenge is the natural response. I wanted Kyle's co-workers to be made accountable for their carelessness. I wanted them to hurt as my son was hurt and as I was hurting.

Blaming is a part of the grieving process and it was not a long stretch for my mind to find many plausible targets for my blame. If there was anything I could have done to bring my son back, I would have done it. However, I knew there was no action I could take that would bring my son back to life and revenge is not what God's Word teaches.

Forgiveness was not something that I felt, it was a decision I had to make over and over again. Part of what helped me make that decision was knowing that Kyle, who is now living in Heaven with Jesus, would want me to forgive.

While he was alive on earth, Kyle was a young man full of idealism and a love for justice. He was a potential law student who would have wanted me to pursue legal action and I had to take that into consideration. However, I believe that Kyle, who is now living in the very presence of God, is filled with nothing but loving kindness and forgiveness. He is looking at the big picture and seeing how God is using this tragedy for eternal good. (Romans 8:28)

I do not have it in me, in my nature, to forgive such a horrible offense. Only God can remove the hatred from my heart, but I must be willing. I held onto my hatred and blame for a long time as a way of holding onto my son. In time, I realized that staying in the past was not going to keep me near Kyle. He is not in the past. He has gone on ahead. To get to where Kyle is, I have to keep moving forward and Heavenward.

Forgive Everyone

"And when you stand praying if you hold anything against anyone, forgive them, so that your Father in Heaven may forgive you your sins." Mark 11:25

The Lord's Prayer, the prayer that Jesus gave us as a pattern of how to pray, includes the request "forgive us our debts as we forgive our debtors." In some Bible versions the word trespasses is used, either way it means offenses, or sins. Jesus told a parable illustrating how Christians, because we have been forgiven our very large debts by God, are to forgive the smaller debts owed to us by others. (Matthew 18:21-35)

I had to choose to forgive the unforgiveable when I didn't feel like forgiving. When my mind got caught up in rumination over all the careless mistakes that were made and the irreparable pain and damage that had been caused I could feel the rage boiling up in me, time after time. I knew I could not forgive on my own. I needed God's supernatural strength. I had to settle in my own mind and heart that God is ultimately in control of all things.

I read a book about the Amish schoolhouse shootings that took place in 2006 and how the parents of the slain Amish children, along with the entire Amish community, offered forgiveness to the family of the killer who had also killed himself. They took the above scripture very seriously and literally and believed that if they did not forgive others, God would not forgive them

It's difficult to let go of a hurt against myself and infinitely harder to let go of a hurt against my child. God has given me such an overwhelming protective love for my children. When my instincts tell me to fight, I need to meekly forgive. I need to forgive all the wrongs that were done to my son because God's Word tells me to and because it is the only way I can replace the darkness in my soul with God's light.

Prayer: Father God, You know forgiveness is too hard for me to do on my own. I just can't muster up the feeling of forgiveness. Help me begin by making the choice to forgive, and then making that choice again and again for as long as it takes. I desire to be obedient to You and to Your Word. I'm desperate for Your help. Amen.

Overcome Evil with Good

"Do not take revenge, my dear friends, but leave room for God's wrath, for it is written: 'It is mine to avenge; I will repay,' says the Lord. Do not be overcome with evil but overcome evil with good." Romans 12:19, 21

The previously mentioned Amish school shooting incident also illustrates what can happen when an injured person is unable to forgive. The perpetrator was a husband and father who was struggling with grief due to the death of his daughter. He was angry with God for letting her die and his violent act was meant as an act of retribution against God. It had been several years since his daughter had died and he and his wife were raising other children, but he was so overcome with anger and bitterness that he committed the horrific mass murder. He was overcome by evil and the outcome was even more evil. His actions brought even more pain and suffering to his family and to many other families.

The Bible teaches us that we are in a spiritual battle. There are forces of evil that are hell-bent on destroying us. The bible tells us to be strong in the Lord and in His mighty power. **"For our struggle is not against flesh and blood, but against the rulers, against the authorities, against the powers of this dark world and against the spiritual forces of evil in the Heavenly realms." (Eph. 6:12)**

Knowing there are dark forces warring for my soul gives me resolve to never give in to thoughts of seeking revenge on people who have hurt me.

The types of spiritual weapons the Bible tells me to use to defend myself against spiritual forces of evil are "...**the belt of truth, the breastplate of righteousness, the gospel of peace, the shield of faith, the helmet of salvation, and the sword of the Spirit, which is the word of God." (Eph. 6:13-18)**

Prayer: Father God, You are mighty in power! I pray You will equip me and my family for spiritual battles by covering us with your armor as we fight to overcome evil with good. Please protect us during this time of grieving when we are especially vulnerable. Thank you that we do not fight alone and our victory is assured because You are with us. Keep us from seeking revenge, knowing it's Your job and not ours. Amen.

Do Not Judge

"Do not judge, or you too will be judged. For in the same way you judge others, you will be judged, and with the measure you use, it will be measured to you." Matthew 7:1-2

This scripture tells us we will be judged in the same way we judge others. Most of us have different criteria for judging our own mistakes and judging the mistakes of others. We tend to make excuses for our own sin while holding others completely accountable.

Blaming someone is judging them to be guilty. I did a lot of blaming and I had many targets for my blame, including my son and myself. If my son had gone to a doctor he would not have died. I knew he had been having stomach aches and I suspected ulcers because of his job stress, his intense nature, and medications he was taking. I was angry with my son for not taking better care of himself and I was angry with myself for not ensuring he went to see a doctor.

You would think it would be easy to forgive my son, after all, he suffered greatly. But I was angry that by his carelessness he brought this immense sadness on our family. He was in Heaven immersed in God's love, joy and peace while we were down here grieving our hearts out.

One of the most perplexing questions I had during this time was how our free will (our human ability to make meaningful choices) works in conjunction with God's sovereignty. I needed to know whose fault this was!

I read much on this topic and have discovered a plethora of opinions and theologies. I've come to accept, although not completely understand, that both of these seemingly contradictory things are simultaneously true. People have the God-given ability to make choices that produce outcomes AND God is in control. People are responsible and will be held accountable for their actions AND God is sovereign over everything that happens. God is never unconcerned or unable to act. He can intervene in any situation and bring about the outcome He determines is best.

Prayer: Father God, I pray You will give me a child-like faith that trusts You even when I don't understand Your ways. I pray You will give me the grace to keep from judging and blaming, knowing You are ultimately in control of everything that happens in the lives of Your people. Help me to trust You. Amen.

Get Rid of all Bitterness

"Get rid of all bitterness, rage and anger, brawling and slander, along with every form of malice. Be kind and compassionate to one another, forgiving each other, just as in Christ God forgave you." Ephesians 4:31-32

This scripture tells us the way to get rid of our negative feelings, emotions, and actions toward the people who hurt us is to be kind to them and to forgive them as God has forgiven us.

The people who had a part in letting my son die were not the only people I needed to forgive. In my grief I was easily hurt and offended by thoughtless comments and actions. I was self-focused, bitter, filled with anger and self-pity, and deeply depressed.

Even though I wanted isolation, it still hurt that friends avoided me. I think many people just didn't know what to say to me and so, feeling awkward and afraid to say the wrong thing, they stayed away. I don't think it's a lack of compassion – it's not that they can't imagine or empathize with the pain of losing a child – I think it's because they can. All moms know the worst thing that can happen is to lose a child. I knew it before it happened to me.

Also, a grieving, depressed, self-focused person is not much fun to be with. But God gave me a couple of brave and loyal friends who continued to call me, send cards, and meet me for lunch dates and walks. And Jesus became my closest, most faithful, and most trusted friend.

In many ways it was good that not too many people were brave enough to come around because it forced me to rely on Jesus alone. After all, He was the only One who could offer me the healing and comfort I needed.

I hope I have learned how I can be a loyal and comforting friend to others who are suffering severe emotional trauma and that I will not hesitate to get in the trenches with them.

Prayer: Father God, please soothe my hurts, help me to get rid of all my bitterness and to overlook offenses. If it's just you and me walking this road together, I'm good with that. The Bible teaches that You, Jesus are the friend that sticks closer than a brother. Thank you for being my faithful friend. Amen.

Don't Take God's Place

"But Joseph said to them, 'Don't be afraid. Am I in the place of God? You intended to harm me, but God intended it for good to accomplish what is now being done, the saving of many lives." Genesis 50:19-20

Joseph was brutally mistreated by his brothers and spent several decades suffering in prison and in slavery because of his brothers' actions. But in this amazing story of redemption, we see how God used Joseph's brothers' evil intent to bring about the good that He intended all along - to preserve the family lineage of Jesus.

Joseph was deeply wounded and he struggled to forgive his brothers. Ultimately, Joseph recognized the good that God had brought from his tragic life and believed that God was sovereign over it all.

Reading the story of Joseph's life (Genesis 37-50) and seeing how God redeemed the unfair suffering he endured helps me when I think about all the things that seem unfair in my life and my son's life. People may intend to harm us, but God intends everything He allows into our lives for our eternal good.

I cannot yet see the good, or guess what it might be. From my current perspective, there is no good God can bring about that will make up for the loss of my son. I'm still living in my self-centered, sinful skin and my wounds are fresh. I just can't imagine what good God could bring about that would be worth all the suffering my family is having to endure.

The Bible doesn't tell us if Joseph ever wavered in his faith during all the years he spent in a dark, rat-infested prison, or if he stubbornly continued to believe God would bring about all He had promised. Later, when Joseph had already seen the good God had brought about, he still struggled to forgive his brothers. This tells me that even if I knew the good God intended to bring about from my family's tragedy it would not ease my pain. One day, when I am in Heaven, I may look back on these unbearable years and praise God for His wisdom and foresight.

Prayer: Father God, help me to believe You are working all things together for eternal good, and that you will sustain me and my family during this dark time of suffering. Amen.

Pray for People Who Hurt You

"Jesus said, 'Father, forgive them, for they do not know what they are doing.'" Luke 23:34

The story of Joseph is an excellent illustration of God bringing about good from the evil actions of people, but the Bible's ultimate example of good coming from evil is the crucifixion of Christ. God intended it to happen. It was prophesied in the Old Testament. Jesus went to the cross willingly and laid down His life of His own accord because it was the only way to save us. (John 10:18)

Jesus asked God to forgive those who nailed Him to the cross. As He was hanging there dying, Jesus prayed for the souls of His tormentors. He asked God to forgive them on the basis that they didn't know what they were doing. (Luke 23:34)

Is it possible that when people hurt us, and when we hurt others, we don't know what we're doing? Are we so self-centered that we really cannot understand how hurtful our words and actions can be? Perhaps so many of Jesus' teachings have to do with having compassion for others because it doesn't come naturally to us.

In His sermon on the mount, Jesus said, **"Love your enemies and pray for those who persecute you." (Matthew 5:44)** He warned against only loving those who love you, saying even the tax collectors and pagans do that. (Matthew 5:46-47)

The apostle Paul says something similar in his letter to the Romans. **"Bless those who persecute you; bless and do not curse. Rejoice with those who rejoice; mourn with those who mourn." (Romans 12:14-15)**

Having this kind of empathy and compassion for others is not easy for me when it's contrary to how I am feeling. Not many people have been willing to mourn with me, and during my mourning I have not been willing to rejoice with people who have been rejoicing. The best way to gain compassion for others is to pray for them like Jesus did.

Prayer: Father God, please forgive every person who has hurt me and help me to have compassion on them on the basis that they did not know what they were doing. Please give the people I've hurt compassion and forgiveness toward me too. Help us all to follow Jesus' example of radical love and forgiveness. Amen.

Find Rest for Your Soul

"Come to me, all who labor and are heavy laden, and I will give you rest. Take my yoke upon you, and learn from me, for I am gentle and lowly in heart, and you will find rest for your souls." Matthew 11:28-29

These are the words of Jesus promising us that when we come to Him with our heavy loads, He will become our burden-bearer and will give us rest for our souls.

About one year after my son died, the worship team at church began to play and sing the hymn, "It is Well with My Soul." I felt anger and bitterness surging up inside of me. I told my husband we needed to leave immediately. "It will never be well with my soul," I vehemently proclaimed as I marched across the parking lot.

I recently read about the author of that hymn, Horatio Spafford. He wrote this hymn just a few days after losing all four of his daughters when the ship they were traveling on sunk in the ocean. Really? In just a few days it was already well with his soul?

Not long ago I met a woman whose 4-year-old granddaughter had died by accidental shooting just a few months earlier. She expressed no anger or blame toward the shooter. She trusted that her granddaughter was in Heaven, safe in the arms of Jesus, and that was enough for her. She was sad and her eyes watered when she spoke of her granddaughter, but she had no anger or bitterness. She knew God was going to bring good from her tragedy. Really?

I began feeling there was something wrong with me that kept me grieving in such a hard and bitter way for so long – something I was missing that I needed so desperately to grasp. These other Christ-followers had something I didn't have – they had peaceful souls.

Like the helpless cripple by the pool at Bethesda (John 5), I needed to answer Jesus' question, "Do you want to be healed?"

In my grief, I've been holding on tightly… but to the wrong things. I need to let go of all my negative emotions and instead hold onto Jesus.

Prayer: Lord Jesus, I am heavy-laden with grief and I need you to bear my burden. I am desperate for the soul rest that I can only get from You. Please make me willing to be healed. I want to be yoked with You. I want your peace. Amen.

Week Three

THINK OF HEAVEN

The grief a parent experiences over the loss of a child is different than that of other losses because we are supposed to die first and we are supposed to take care of our children. From the time our child is born we do all we can to keep them safe and alive. Regular feedings, vitamins, well-baby checks, medicine when they're sick, and child safety seats. We enroll them in the best schools, take them to church, the dentist, the orthodontist, the dermatologist. We give, we invest, we nurture, we protect. The love God gives us for our children is amazing – so protective and self-sacrificial. So how can God ask us to live through the loss of our child? Haven't we failed to do the primary thing every parent instinctively knows to do – to keep our child alive?

When Kyle was only a few months old, his pediatrician noticed one of his eyes was turned in and referred us to an ophthalmologist who recommended corrective surgery. I agonized over this decision and did all the research I possibly could in those pre-internet days. Ultimately we decided to proceed with the surgery and we had a good result. However, handing my baby over to the nurse to take him into surgery was an exceedingly hard thing to do. I had to trust God to be with my baby in the operating room where I could not go.

It was hard seeing the post-surgery redness and swelling on my precious baby's eyes. It was horrible watching my baby suffer and not being able to relieve his pain. As parents, I'm certain the pain of seeing our children suffer is far worse than suffering ourselves.

When Kyle died, I did not immediately think about myself, my loss and my grief. All I could think about was Kyle's suffering. He was alone when he died. I wondered what it was like for him. (We were told he probably thought he had stomach flu and he probably died in his sleep.)

I thought about all the things Kyle would miss out on. Marriage, children, career – life. He had big plans and he had the intelligence and motivation to make them all happen. Why would God allow such potential to be lost to this world? My son was a good man with so much to contribute.

And what about all the prayers I prayed for Kyle through the years? Did God hear them?

The only way to answer these questions and to make sense of the death of a young person, is to understand and believe that this life is not all there is. Even if we live to be 80 or 90 years old, this life is short in contrast to all of eternity. Kyle has not ceased to exist, he has only ceased to exist here. His body died, but his soul lives with Jesus in Heaven. I don't know specifically what Kyle is doing in Heaven, but I know it is Kingdom work. God is making good use of all of Kyle's wonderful talents. I have always been proud of Kyle and his accomplishments, and I can continue to be proud of him. I know he is serving the Lord with excellence.

God's grace was with Kyle when his body died and Jesus was there to take Kyle's soul to Heaven. Kyle is perfectly loved and has no more anxiety or stress. Kyle is fully and completely himself – all that God created him to be. If Kyle were given the option to come back and live another 60 years, I believe he would decline because of the unsurpassed beauty and excellence of Heaven.

Through the years I have had to relinquish control over my son's life. I have had to learn to trust God to care for him when I couldn't be with him. I don't know when I will next be with my son, but I know he is safe in Heaven and I can trust Jesus to take care of him.

I have had to learn to set my heart and mind on Heaven. When I think of the unfairness of losing my son at such a young age, when the angry and bitter thoughts bombard, and when the overwhelming sadness suffocates, I choose to refocus my emotions and my thoughts on Heaven. Kyle lives there now, with Jesus, and one day I will live there too.

A man whose daughter died told me the secret to getting through all the hard days of grief is to think of Heaven. Learn all you can about Heaven, meditate on Heaven, and anticipate all the goodness that your loved one has there and all that awaits you there too.

Set Your Heart and Mind on Heaven

"Since, then, you have been raised with Christ, set your hearts on things above, where Christ is, seated at the right hand of God. Set your minds on things above, not on earthly things. For you died, and your life is now hidden with Christ in God. When Christ, who is your life, appears, then you also with appear with Him in glory." Colossians 3:1-4

This scripture is part of a letter the apostle Paul wrote to the Colossians to encourage them to behave now as citizens of Heaven.

Because Jesus died for our sins, was resurrected, and ascended to Heaven, all who trust Jesus as their Savior have, in a sense, already been raised along with Him. Our hearts and minds are free to rise above earthly concerns. Our sinful lives are now hidden in His perfect life.

This is a verse I recite to myself when I am feeling overwhelmed with heartache and despair over what has happened and all I have lost. It reminds me to think about Heaven. It reminds me that this life is not all there is, and because I have trusted Jesus as my Savior, Heaven is my home and all my heart desires is there. But even more than that, it reminds me that I don't have to wait until I reach Heaven to enjoy the unsurpassed bliss of Heaven. I can set my heart on it right now. Instead of living in despair with a broken heart, I can let Jesus mend my heart with the assurance of eternal life in Heaven for my son, for myself, and all my family. Setting my heart on Heaven is the same as setting my heart on Jesus. Everything is going to be okay because of Jesus.

This verse instructs me to set not only my heart but also my mind on things above. Things happen every day that will distress me if I let my mind be set on them. Setting my mind instead on the beauty, surety and eternalness of Heaven helps me to tolerate earthly and temporary problems because I understand they are temporary.

Prayer: Lord Jesus, thank you for saving us and assuring us of eternal life in Heaven with You. Give me confidence that, in the end, my family and I will all stand with You on the side of victory. Help me now to put my affection and my intelligence on the eternal things rather than on temporary things. Amen.

Do Not Let Your Heart be Troubled

"Do not let your hearts be troubled. You believe in God; believe also in me. My Father's house has many rooms; if that were not so, would I have told you that I am going there to prepare a place for you? And if I go and prepare a place for you, I will come back and take you to be with me that you also may be where I am." John 14:1-3

Jesus wants us to have untroubled hearts. The cure He prescribes for a troubled heart is belief in God and in Jesus. Belief is faith, and faith is a gift from God. We can ask God to give us more faith – more belief. This is a prayer God will surely answer because it is His will and His desire for us to believe in Him and in His Son, Jesus and to have faith in them.

Jesus said His Father's house has many rooms and He is going there to prepare a place for us. Then He is coming back to take us to be with Him where He lives – in His Father's house.

Jesus will come for us whether our time to go to Heaven is at our death, or when Jesus returns to take His followers into Heaven. Before Jesus comes for us, He will prepare a special place for us – a room in His Father's house.

It helps me to know that although my son's death was a surprise to me and to him, it was not a surprise to Jesus. Before my son died, Jesus had lovingly prepared a place for him in Heaven. There is no better, more joyous, peaceful, or safer place for my son to be. Jesus knows my son better than anyone and he knows what my son likes. He prepared a place for my son that is better than I can imagine, but I do like trying to imagine it.

It helps me to know that Jesus came for my son, comforted him in his pain, and took him directly to Heaven. My son was not alone when he died and he will never be alone again.

Prayer: Jesus, please keep my heart from being troubled. I believe in You! Thank you that you care for my family and I and that you will never leave us. Thank you for preparing a special place for each of us. Thank you that You will come for us when it's our time to go home. Amen.

Consider Your Loved One's Gain

"For to me, to live is Christ and to die is gain. If I am to go on living in the body, this will mean fruitful labor for me. Yet what shall I choose? I do not know! I am torn between the two: I desire to depart and be with Christ, which is better by far;" **Philippians 1:21-23**

The apostle Paul says, as long as he goes on living "in the body" he will work for Christ's Kingdom but when he dies he will consider it a gain. He will go on living either "in the body" or "out of the body." He says it is good to stay in the body and serve the Lord, but it is better by far to depart and be with Christ.

When our loved ones die, it is a great loss for us who are left behind, but for our loved ones who die in Christ it is a gain. They have gained Heaven and immortality and are living in Christ's presence.

It's hard to think of my son's death as his gain. I think of all he left undone here. He was only 24 years old and just beginning his career. He had plans to go to graduate school or law school. He had yet to get married and have children. I think about the daughter-in-law and the grandchildren I will never have. It's hard for me to fathom how it was better for my son to die so young.

It seems my son missed out on a lot of the things that are good in this life, but he also got to fast-forward through a lot of trouble. Life is hard for everyone, filled with disappointment, loss, heartache, pain, suffering, striving and stress. Along with all the good experiences my son missed, there are a lot of bad things he didn't have to experience.

According to Paul, the resurrection of Christ and the assurance of eternal life in Heaven takes the sting out of death. *"Where, O death, is your victory? Where, O death, is your sting?" (1 Cor. 15:55) "Thanks be to God! He gives us the victory through our Lord Jesus Christ." (1 Cor. 15:57)* Death is still an enemy, but it is a defeated enemy.

Prayer: Father God, help me to believe that it is infinitely better to depart and be with Christ. It is Your choice and not mine when I will depart to be with Christ. Help me as long as I am living in the body to live for Christ. Please make my labor fruitful. Amen.

Let God Strengthen Your Heart

*"I was senseless and ignorant; I was a brute beast before you. Yet, I am always with You; You hold me by my right hand. You guide me with Your counsel, and afterward you will take me into glory. Whom have I in Heaven but you? And earth has nothing I desire besides you. My flesh and my heart may fail, but God is the strength of my heart and my portion forever."
Psalm 73:22-26*

This Psalm assures us that God is always with us, holding us, guiding us, and giving us strength. He will walk the rough road of life with us and when life is over, He will take us into glory.

Like the Psalmist, I too behaved like a brute beast toward God. My heart was grieved and my spirit embittered. The hurt in me was so immense that it poured out and was beyond my ability to control. Even God was not exempt from my raging accusations. Yet I was always with God because God was always with me. When my grief blinded me, He took me by the hand and guided me.

Before God took my son to Heaven, earth had a lot of things my heart desired besides God. I've learned that this temporary life is not worthy of my heart's desire because it's temporary.

The only sure thing I have is God. Who else on Heaven or earth is certain to always be with me? I don't know when the people I love may be taken from me. During this volatile life the only thing I can depend on is God.

My flesh and my heart will indeed one day fail, but God has become the strength of my heart. He has replaced my heart's desire for a perfect temporary life with His perfect love and perfect promise of eternity with Him. He has replaced the meager portion with which I was content and He Himself has become my portion.

One day my heart will stop beating and my body will die. My life on earth will be over and every earthly thing will be left behind, but God will continue to be with me.

Prayer: Father God, help me to express all my feelings and emotions to You without sinning against You, for whom have I but You? Hold me by my hand and guide me with your counsel. You are the strength of my heart and my portion forever. Amen

Choose Heavenly Thoughts

"Finally, brothers and sisters, whatever is true, whatever is noble, whatever is right, whatever is pure, whatever is lovely, whatever is admirable – if anything is excellent or praiseworthy – think about such things." Philippians 4:8

God has given us humans the ability to choose what we think about. We can't stop thoughts from entering our mind, but we can choose what we dwell on. We can replace a discouraging thought with an encouraging one. No matter how many things are bad or wrong, there is always something for which to be thankful.

Even when I am overwhelmed with despair, anger and confusion about why God allowed this painful tragedy, I still have one thing for which I can give thanks – my son's salvation. I know my son trusted Jesus as his Savior and he is safe in Heaven. When I am tormented by dark thoughts, I can direct my mind back to thinking about God's sovereign care over my son's life and the promise of all that is yet to come.

What is true…My son is in Heaven with Jesus. There is no brighter, happier, better place for him to be.

What is noble…Jesus paid the price for my son's sins and purchased his salvation.

What is right…Jesus came for my son and took him to Heaven.

What is pure…God's steadfast love. Nothing can ever separate us from His love.

What is lovely…Heaven is a perfect place, no sorrow, crying, or pain.

What is admirable…My son ran his race with perseverance.

What is excellent…One day I will be in Heaven with Jesus and with my son.

What is praiseworthy…God's faithfulness. Our names will never be blotted from the Lamb's book of life.

Prayer: Father God, please keep me mindful of all the things for which I have to be grateful and whenever dark thoughts come into my mind help me to replace them with better, Heavenly thoughts. Amen.

Present Your Requests to God

"Do not be anxious about anything, but in every situation, by prayer and petition, with thanksgiving, present your requests to God. And the peace of God, which transcends all understanding, will guard your hearts and your minds in Christ Jesus." Philippians 4:6-7

This scripture tells us that God's peace transcends understanding. What I think this means is that we can have God's peace without understanding the reason for our adverse circumstances. And we can have God's peace even in the midst of the circumstances that are causing our anxiety. God can give us His peace without changing our situations or our understanding of them. We are instructed to guard our hearts and our minds from the chaos of anxiety with the peace of God. And we are to receive His supernatural peace through prayer.

Many times in my grief I have desperately needed God's peace. When I feel anxious, I pray constantly, begging God to give me the assurance I need that He is in control and my son's death was not random and is not meaningless. I need the peace that only God can give me. Often as I pray I can feel anxiety melting away even though nothing has changed.

The pattern this scripture gives us for our prayers is to present our requests with thanksgiving. I searched for things for which to give God thanks and was surprised to find several. My son trusted Jesus as his Savior; our family attended a great church together for over 10 years; at that church we all came to have saving faith in Jesus Christ.

In addition, I am thankful for God's promises in the Bible. God has promised to never leave us nor forsake us. He has promised eternal life in Heaven for all who will believe in His Son, Jesus Christ. He has promised to faithfully love us with His unfailing love.

One day I may understand all of God's ways that are unfathomable to me right now, but I don't have to wait until then to receive God's peace.

Prayer: Father God, thank you that you desire that I not be anxious and you give me the antidote for my anxiety. Even though I continue to lack understanding, my broken heart and weary mind can be soothed and protected as you fill me with Your supernatural peace. May it be so. Amen.

Set Your Heart at Rest

"This is how we know that we belong to the truth and how we set our hearts at rest in His presence: If our hearts condemn us, we know that God is greater than our hearts, and He knows everything." 1 John 3:19-20

This verse tells us that God is greater than our condemning hearts and greater than our guilt. He has forgiven us through the atoning work of Christ, and He knows everything about us.

There is a lot of guilt involved in grief. I've read that if you can cut out the guilt you will cut the pain of your grief in half. I was told by a professional counselor that everyone feels guilty when someone dies. I have found in talking to other parents who have lost children that they always feel they could have done something that would have prevented their child's death. I can see how unrealistic this is in every case, except of course my own. I am tortured by thoughts of what I failed to do.

If we live long enough, we will live with regrets. We are prone to rethink, rehash, and ruminate over our mistakes and regret we didn't make different choices. Many of us are inclined toward feeling guilty over everything that happens and may have a distorted view of how much control we have over other people's choices, feelings, and actions.

Feeling guilty is not always bad. The above scripture tells us it is one way we can have confirmation that we belong to God. If our hearts condemn us – if we feel guilt and remorse over our prideful and self-centered ways – it's proof that God's Holy Spirit lives in us and is at battle with our innate sinful nature.

When we are grieving we are vulnerable and need to be careful not to fall victim to false guilt that comes from Satan, who the Bible calls "the accuser." (Rev. 12:10) We should ask God to bring to mind the things for which we truly need to repent, then ask Him to forgive us with the full assurance that He will. (1 John 1:9)

Prayer: Father God, I repent of all the wrong things I have done. Show me the specific sins for which I need to repent. Protect me from false guilt. Thank you for the assurance that you love me and forgive me even though You know everything about me. Amen.

Week Four

RELY ON GOD

When Kyle died, the question that most tormented me and most demanded an answer was, "Why?" It just seemed so senseless, so random, and so very, very unfair.

"Why did God allow this to happen?" I prayed for Kyle, as I did for all of my sons – that God would protect him. I believed God had good plans for my son and that He would ensure they were carried out. I believed God was all-powerful, all-knowing, good and loving and that He was watching over all of my sons when I could not. I relied on these things. I relied on God.

But now it seemed God had let me down. That He wasn't reliable after all. How could God be all the things I believed Him to be in light of what had happened? Was this God's plan for Kyle's life or had God lost control? Did God cause this, or did He just allow it? Is there a difference? Going forward, can I still rely on God and His sovereign control over the lives of my family members?

Scripture tells us that sometimes God takes His children home to spare them from evil in this life. (Isaiah 57:1-2) It also tells us, *"...all the days ordained for me were written in your book before one of them came to be." (Psalm 139:16)* And, *"Precious in the sight of the Lord is the death of His saints." (Psalm 116:15)*

These scriptures illustrate God's control and care over the death of those who belong to Him in Christ. He doesn't take their deaths lightly, He always has good purposes, and He always has a plan. But there is at least one man who was able to change God's plan through fervent and heart-felt prayer. A man named Hezekiah. (2 Kings 20:1-11) Hezekiah was told by the Lord that he was about to die. Hezekiah begged God for more time and God granted him another 15 years.

I didn't know that Kyle was about to die, but I wondered if I could have convinced God to give him more time if I had been more diligent in prayer, if I had known to specifically pray for it. Then I wondered if perhaps God had already given me extra time with my son.

Reflecting back, there were several times when Kyle was in high school when it seemed God rescued him from illnesses and accidents.

When Kyle was 15 years old and learning to drive, he was merging onto the freeway and there was a close call with a semi-truck. I was in the passenger seat and it seemed a collision was unavoidable and that somehow our car passed right through the truck.

After getting his license, Kyle was driving solo and had an accident that totaled his car, yet he walked away unhurt.

In his sophomore year of high school Kyle developed an extremely serious and potentially life-threatening thyroid condition that was resolved with several months of medical treatment and prayer.

In his senior year of high school, Kyle was having some leg pain and found a lump on a bone in his leg. There was a shadow on an x-ray and his doctor suspected bone cancer. Kyle was referred to a specialist who determined the lump was a benign bone spur. We had prayed a lot during the time between appointments and Kyle and I were both certain that God had intervened and healed him.

Perhaps God had already saved Kyle many times and graciously granted me more time with my son.

I cannot understand why God allowed Kyle to die at such a young age. But I can be grateful for the 24 years I had with my son and the eternity I will still have with him in Heaven.

A friend whose son died told me she thinks of this time that her son is absent from her life as being in parenthesis. If life were a sentence there would be all the time before her son died and all the time they will have together in eternity. This painful time would be in parenthesis – no more than a side note.

I'm certain that I'm currently living out the most difficult years of my life. I've never been less competent. I cannot rely on my own abilities to sustain me and to ultimately make things right. Even though I don't understand why God allowed my son to leave this life so soon, I know God has raised my son to eternal life in Heaven. I know I can rely on God to carry me through this time of grief and, one day, to right every wrong. God is still all the things I have always known Him to be – and exceedingly more.

Rely on God

"We do not want you to be uninformed, brothers and sisters, about the troubles we experienced in the province of Asia. We were under great pressure, far beyond our ability to endure, so that we despaired of life itself. Indeed, we felt we had received the sentence of death. But this happened that we might not rely on ourselves but on God, who raises the dead."
2 Corinthians 1:8-9

God probably will not tell us why He has allowed suffering in our specific circumstance, however, in the Bible He reveals some of the reasons He allows, and even brings suffering into our lives.

The apostle Paul wanted the Corinthians to know about the trouble he and his companions experienced and to understand that their troubles were so great that they were unable to endure and wanted to die. Paul goes on to tell them the reason they were allowed to suffer as they did. It was so they would learn to rely on God.

We are self-reliant people. We strive for independence and self-promotion. We like being in control of all things at all times. It feels good and it feels secure, but we are only fooling ourselves. We are not in control. We are not God. We do not know all things, control all things, and are not able to be all places at all times. Do you really want to rely on yourself? Wouldn't you rather rely on God, who has the power to raise the dead?

I can relate to the emotions Paul expresses in this scripture because my grief has been far beyond my ability to endure. I am no longer relying on myself or my own ability because I am neither reliable nor able. I am helpless to do anything for my son. I cannot raise the dead. My hope is in God, who has raised my son from death into eternal life.

Prayer: Father God, You know all the things that have died in me. Some things, such as self-reliance are better left dead. Some things, such as a willing spirit need to be raised. I pray you will do a resurrection in my heart, mind, and spirit, giving me the strength to go on living all the days You have ordained for me. I am relying on You. Amen.

Rely on God's Unfailing Love

"Love never fails. For now we see only a reflection as in a mirror; then we shall see face to face. Now I know in part; then I shall know fully, even as I am fully known. And now these three remain: faith, hope and love. But the greatest of these is love." Cor. 13:8,12,13

God is perfect and God's love is perfect. This scripture tells us that we don't even know what perfect love looks like because we cannot see clearly. Our sin is a fog that keeps us from seeing in full – we only see in part. The difference between how we perceive God's love now and how we will perceive it in Heaven is the difference between looking in a foggy mirror and looking into a real face. One day we will meet God face to face and we will comprehend His perfect love for us.

Because we humans are not perfect, our love isn't perfect. Sometimes we get hurt and sometimes we get mad. This is how human love and relationships go. Imperfect people love imperfectly.

There were times when my son and I had disagreements. When we were in the midst of discord, I often poured out my broken heart in prayer for our relationship. During those times, I would meditate on God's promise that "Love never fails." I understood this as God's promise to me that as long as I continued to love my son everything would be okay. Love would triumph. Our relationship might falter, but it would not break … because of love.

God's love never fails because it never comes to an end. Neither will the love God has given me for my son ever end. Death has not stopped me from loving my son. Faith, hope, and love remain in my heart. Death could not take them from me because death is not the end. God has kept my faith, hope and love alive and His word assures me my son is alive.

Another way God's love cannot fail is, unlike human love, it is not dependent on anything we do or don't do. Only God can love like that.

Prayer: Father God, thank you for your perfect love that will never fail and is not dependent on human performance. Please allow faith, hope and love to remain in my heart. Amen.

Be Secure in God's Love

"For I am convinced that neither death nor life, neither angels nor demons, neither the present nor the future, nor any powers, neither height nor depth, nor anything else in all creation, will be able to separate us from the love of God that is in Christ Jesus our Lord." Romans 8:38-39

According to this scripture nothing can separate us from God's love. Nothing. Not even us. Because we did not earn God's love we cannot un-earn it. God chose us to belong to Him and He will never un-choose us. Once we belong to God there is nothing we can do or fail to do that can stop Him from loving us. Everything that God does is because of His great love for us.

This verse assures me my son was never outside of the protective embrace of God's sovereign, steadfast love. This is a promise I clung to immediately after my son's death and this verse is one that was spoken at his memorial service. What I needed to know more than anything was that my son was with God.

When something goes wrong we look for a cause. We believe if something bad happens to us it is punishment for something we have done. This is not true for God's children. God does not punish His children because He has already punished Jesus in their place. (God does discipline us but that's different than punishment. See Hebrews 12:10-11)

Death is not punishment for a Christian because death is the way God brings His children home to Heaven – into His very presence.

In the early days of my grief I struggled to know why this tragedy happened. In analyzing all that went wrong that contributed to my son's death I found many instances where a different human choice would have yielded different results. Yet, in every instance, God could have intervened and saved my son's life. Even though it is impossible for me to understand, I have to accept that God determined this was best for my son.

Prayer: Father God, thank you for Your love that is not dependent on me or anything I do or don't do, but on what Jesus has already done. You are faithful, long-suffering, patient, merciful, gracious, and mighty to save. Please keep me secure in Your love. Amen.

Be Assured of Salvation

"My sheep listen to my voice; I know them, and they follow me. I give them eternal life, and they shall never perish; no one can snatch them out of my hand. My Father, who has given them to me, is greater than all; no one can snatch them out of my Father's hand. I and the Father are one." John 10:27-30

Like the previous scripture in Romans, this scripture shows that our salvation is secure in Christ. The day we put our lives in Christ's hands it's a sealed deal. We are Christ's sheep, given to Him by the Father. As we are in Christ's hand, we are also in God's hand because Jesus and God are One.

Earlier in John 10, Jesus says He lays down His life for His sheep because He is their Shepherd. He contrasts this to a hired hand who leaves the sheep when he sees a wolf coming. Jesus says He would never do that because He is The Good Shepherd.

When Jesus died on the cross, He died in place of all people who would trust in Him, paying the price for our sins so that we never have to. When we put our trust into His nail-scarred hands we are assured He will never let go, even if someone or something tries to force us from His hand. Any wolves that come along are already defeated.

These are great promises for every believer, and assurances I really needed to cling to. My son was given eternal life through his belief in Jesus Christ so he will never perish. He walked right from life in this world into eternal life with Christ. There was nothing that could pry my son from God's grip and there is nothing that can wrench me from His hand either.

Doubt, discouragement, and depression are enemies that have stalked me in my grief and tried to pull me away from God. Though they weaken me, they only strengthen God's hold on me.

Prayer: Jesus, You are The Good Shepherd. You laid down Your life for Your sheep and Your sheep are safe in Your care. There is no safer place to be than in Your flock. No predator can take me from You. You never abandoned my loved one and You will never abandon me. Thank you. Amen.

Trust In God's Purposes

"The righteous perish, and no one takes it to heart; the devout are taken away, and no one understands that the righteous are taken away to be spared from evil."
Isaiah 57:1

My Bible notes tell me this verse refers to King Josiah who humbled himself before the Lord and thus was spared the judgment that was to come by being "gathered to his fathers, and buried in peace so that his eyes would not see disaster." (2 Kings 22:19-20)

We can learn from this verse that when the righteous (those who have been made righteous by their faith in Christ) perish, it's not punishment and it's not random. God takes them away to spare them from the evil in this world.

We cannot know or understand why God chooses to do things the way He does. There are many ways God could have both protected my son from evil and kept him here in the world.

This verse says that no one takes it to heart and no one understands. No one takes to heart the danger in the world and the coming judgment for evil. No one understands that death to a Christian is going home to peace and rest.

There is another sense in which it seems no one takes the death of the devout to heart – they do not expect it to happen to them or their loved ones. My family and I are ordinary people living ordinary lives. If this happened to us, it can happen to anyone. Please take it to heart.

Matthew 24:37-39 describes the normal things people were doing before the flood and says it will be the same way before Christ appears. In verse 44 Jesus says, *"So you also must be ready, because the Son of Man will come at an hour when you do not expect him."*

Prayer: Father God, we are all living with the effects of evil in this world and coming home to You will always be merciful. Thank you for the assurance of knowing that You determine when Your children come home. Death is never random or meaningless. Help me to trust in Your purposes. Amen

Expect Trouble

"In this world you will have trouble. But take heart! I have overcome the world." John 16:33

When the time was drawing near for Jesus' persecution, he gave the above warning and promise to His disciples. He knew what the future held for them. He knew they would abandon and betray Him after His arrest and that later on they would be persecuted and martyred for their faith.

Jesus said these words to His disciples to encourage them not to be discouraged by the things that were about to happen. Jesus' words of encouragement are for us too. We are certain to have trouble in this world. We are to expect it and be ready for it. But we are to take heart (not be anxious or frightened) because Christ has overcome the world. He has defeated the power of sin and death.

The apostle Peter wrote, *"Beloved, do not be surprised at the fiery trial when it comes upon you to test you, as though something strange were happening to you. But rejoice insofar as you share Christ's sufferings, that you may also rejoice and be glad when His glory is revealed." (1 Peter 4:12)*

The apostle Paul writes something similar to the Romans, telling them that as Christ's followers they are to rejoice in their suffering because *"suffering produces perseverance, perseverance, character; and character, hope." (Romans 5:3-4)*

Because Christ has defeated sin, sin cannot defeat us. But Christ's victory does more than neutralize sin. It takes the consequences of sin (suffering) and uses it to transform the Christian's character and make him more like Christ. Because of Christ's victory, we are able to rejoice knowing our suffering will develop Christ-like character in us.

We don't get to choose whether or not to suffer. The only choice we get is how to react to the unavoidable suffering that life will bring.

Prayer: Thank you, Jesus, that You have defeated the world and turned the consequences of sin around so that suffering brings about good qualities in the Christian. Help us to be prepared for trouble in this life, knowing that sin and suffering are normal parts of the Christian life. Amen.

Rely on God's Keeping Power

"May God himself, the God of peace, sanctify you through and through. May your whole spirit, soul and body be kept blameless at the coming of our Lord Jesus Christ. The one who calls you is faithful, and he will do it." 1 Thess. 5:23-24

This verse comes from the apostle Paul's letter to the Thessalonians and in it Paul is assuring them there is no need to worry about whether they will be sufficiently holy and blameless at the coming of the Lord because it is not up to them. God is faithful and He will surely make it happen.

If we had to sanctify ourselves and keep ourselves blameless we would have great cause for concern because we could never do it.

In Paul's letter to the Philippians, he gives similar reassurance. *"...(be) confident of this, that he who began a good work in you will carry it on to completion until the day of Christ Jesus." (Phil. 1:6)*

Paul also writes to the Ephesians to reassure them of the certainty of their salvation. *"In Him you also, when you heard the word of truth, the gospel of your salvation, and believed in Him, were sealed with the promised Holy Spirit..." (Eph. 1:13)*

The Thessalonians, the Philippians, the Ephesians, and all of us who call Jesus our Lord can have confidence that God, who saved us, will never let us go and that we are most certain to inherit eternal life in Heaven with Jesus.

Paul assures Timothy that God's faithfulness to us does not depend on our faithfulness to Him. *"...if we are faithless, He remains faithful, for He cannot disown Himself." (2 Tim. 2:13)*

God knows us. He knows our sinfulness and the struggles we have because of our pride. In Psalm 103 we are told, *"...He does not treat us as our sins deserve or repay us according to our iniquities," (verse 10) "...for He knows how we are formed, He remembers that we are dust." (verse 14)*

Prayer: Father God, thank you for giving me so many assurances in Your word that our salvation is kept safe in Your strong and loving hands. Thank you for remembering that we are dust. Give me confident faith in Your keeping power. Amen.

45

Week Five

INVEST IN ETERNITY

Jesus taught that where we put our treasure reveals where our heart is. (Matthew 6:19-21) Because so much of my heart is in Heaven with Kyle I want to invest there. The way to invest in Heaven is by doing things that have eternal significance. Jesus said that even a cup of cold water given in His name will be rewarded in Heaven. (Matthew 10:42)

The Bible tells us that we are saved from eternal punishment for our sins, and for an eternity of blessings and rewards, by God's grace through our faith in Jesus Christ. But Jesus also taught us, by word and by example, that we should do good to others out of our love for Him. When we care for "the least of these," (Matthew 25:40) it's as though we are caring for Jesus. There will be rewards in Heaven for good works that are done in Jesus' name.

Not long after Kyle went to Heaven, I had the thought that perhaps any good thing that happened because of Kyle's tragic death would somehow be credited to Kyle. If any of Kyle's friends or family members became new believers or more committed Christians or in any way grew in their faith or lived a better life because of the sobering reality that life can end at any moment, that would be to Kyle's credit.

There is a strong desire for many bereaved people, especially parents, to do good in their loved one's memory. It seems to somehow redeem some of the pain and insure their child is remembered. And taking purposeful action helps to pull us from our all-consuming, self-focused despair.

Some grieving parents that I know have started scholarship funds, set up charitable foundations, and contributed to grief support programs.

My husband and I have done many things in Kyle's memory and hope and plan to do many more as God leads us to more opportunities. We became sponsors to several children in third-world countries through the Rafiki Foundation and World Vision; we raised money for clean water in Africa by running an 8K race; we purchased and donated children's books to a Rafiki school library in Africa; and we have donated to our son's favorite charities.

Our priorities have changed. We desire less for worldly goods and seek to live simpler lives so we are able to spend less and give more. We want to invest less in this temporary life and more in what is eternal. We understand how short life is and we understand the Bible's teaching to keep from working for things that won't last. Everything on earth will be destroyed one day. (2 Peter 3:10) When we work for big houses, nice cars and elaborate vacations, we are being short-sighted. Why work for things that won't last when we can work for things that will last for all eternity?

Our work until Jesus comes is to help people to know Him so that they will be saved for eternity. We help people to know Jesus by showing them His love. The Bible teaches the religion that God accepts as pure and faultless is to care for widows and orphans in distress. (James 1:27)

In his short life, Kyle stored up plenty of his own treasure in Heaven. He went on several mission trips to Mexico to build homes for the poor. He donated money to charities. He spoke openly of his Christian faith. He was a good and loyal friend as many of his friends testified at his memorial service. He had a compassionate spirit, a generous nature, and was a hard worker, striving for excellence with all his God-given talents and abilities.

Early on in my grief, I may have been striving too hard to bring about good from my loss. Romans 8:28 says, ***"And we know that in all things God works for the good of those who love Him, who have been called according to His purpose."*** It is God who will bring about the good. I should do all the good work God leads me to do, but it is God who does the leading.

I believe some of the best treasure we store up in Heaven is our submission to God's sanctification process in us and our obedience to God's Word. Perhaps every time we forgive someone we don't want to forgive; hold back a cutting remark; and refrain from gossip, it's credited to our account in the Heavenly ledgers.

Oh, I hope so strongly that my son can see the hard things I am doing and is proud of me. I hope so deeply that he knows how much he is loved and missed. As I send up my treasure to Heaven, I'm sending my love up to him.

Store Up Treasure in Heaven

"Do not store up for yourselves treasures on earth, where moths and vermin destroy, and where thieves break in and steal. But store up for yourselves treasures in Heaven, where moths and vermin do not destroy, and where thieves do not break in and steal. For where your treasure is, there your heart will be also." Matthew 6:19-21

Earthly treasure is prone to destruction and theft, but the treasure we store up in Heaven is kept safe and cannot be lost. The currencies we have to spend in this life are our time, our talent, and our money. When we spend them to help others we are storing our treasure in Heaven.

When we are hurting, it seems counter-intuitive that we should help others. But by God's perfect and unfathomable design, when we help others it helps us even more.

Just after the one-year anniversary of my son's death, a good friend faced her own tragedy when her husband died. I so desperately wanted to help my friend that I stepped out of my self-imposed isolation to work in her small business for several months while she took time off to grieve. It helped me to have a place to go and work to do. It helped me to have interactions with people.

A few months later I stepped out even further and went to Rwanda, Africa for one month to work at an orphanage and school with the Rafiki Foundation. I fell in love with the children there and when I was laughing and playing with them I felt joy in my heart again.

God used my pain to give me compassion for others who were hurting. And then as I reached out to help them He began to heal me. Only God is wise enough to know the way to begin healing is to begin helping. And only God is powerful enough to orchestrate the circumstances to match up hurting hearts.

Prayer: Father God, thank you for the assurance of salvation through faith in Christ. The good works I do are not to earn a place in Heaven, they are to be obedient to Your word. They are not to bring glory to myself or to my loved one, but to glorify You and to show Your love to hurting people. Thank you for using me to help others and for healing me in the process. Amen.

Anticipate Heaven

"As it is written: 'What no eye has seen, what no ear has heard, and what no human mind has conceived' — the things God has prepared for those who love him — these are the things God has revealed to us by his Spirit. The Spirit searches all things, even the deep things of God." 1 Corinthians 2:9-10

This scripture tells us that God reveals things to us by His Spirit that our human minds could not otherwise conceive. We can only understand spiritual things by the power of the Holy Spirit.

There have been several precious times in my life when God has given me an assurance of His presence. I can only describe these indescribable moments in time as a feeling of pure, supernatural joy when I have KNOWN, in my spirit, that God is REAL.

One summer night several months after our son had gone to Heaven, my husband and I were out for an evening walk. There was a beautiful sunset and the light playing off the trees was magical. It started to get dark and fireflies began appearing. There were little flashes of light here and there. As we continued on toward home it got darker and more fireflies appeared around us. And then in an instant, we were completely surrounded by countless flickering lights. We both stopped and caught our breath, and wide-eyed, looked all around in wonder. Without saying a word we both understood that we were feeling God's presence in our spirits along with the closeness of our son. For a brief moment in time it was as if God had lifted the veil that separates our physical world from the spiritual world and let us be a part of what was happening on the other side. It was indescribably beautiful and peaceful. We both felt God communicating to us that He had our son and all was well.

There are many beautiful things in this seen world, and even more in the unseen world. The things in the unseen world we cannot know except when God reveals them to us by His Spirit.

Prayer: Father God, thank You for revealing Yourself to us in the beauty of nature. I pray for even more glimpses into the Heavenly realms. I thank You for the beauty in this temporary world and the unsurpassed beauty in the eternal world. Help us to joyfully anticipate all that You have prepared for us. Amen.

Look Forward to Christ's Return

"According to the Lord's word, we tell you that we who are still alive, who are left until the coming of the Lord, will certainly not precede those who have fallen asleep. For the Lord himself will come down from Heaven, with a loud command, with the voice of the archangel and with the trumpet call of God, and the dead in Christ will rise first. After that, we who are still alive and are left will be caught up together with them in the clouds to meet the Lord in the air. And so we will be with the Lord forever. Therefore encourage one another with these words." 1 Thess. 4:15-18

The apostle Paul wrote the above words to the Thessalonians to dispel their concerns that their loved ones who had already died would miss out on Jesus' return. Paul states that it is according to the Lord's word that those who have died in Christ will rise first, before those who are still alive. Since we know our loved one's souls are already in Heaven, it is their resurrected bodies that will rise and be reunited with their souls, and then those who are left will meet the Lord and their loved ones in the air.

We should be like children waiting for Christmas morning as we wait for Jesus' return. We should be giddy with anticipation. It could happen at any moment. We are to be encouraged by the certainty of Jesus' return and are to encourage others by talking about it.

If I am alive at Christ's return, the first time I will see my son again will be in the air with Jesus, and then we will be with the Lord forever. I am watching for the Lord's return. I am listening for the loud command, the voice of the archangel, and the trumpet call of God. When Jesus returns it will be the end of this world filled with sorrows and the beginning of a glorious eternity. We will rejoice and no one will be able to take away our joy. It is something I can look forward to with certainty.

Prayer: Father God, life is hard for me right now. Thank you for the promise that Jesus will return, and it may be any day. I pray You will encourage my heart with the surety of Jesus' return and you will help me to encourage others. I look forward to eternity with You. Amen.

Believe Heaven is Better

"Better is one day in your courts than a thousand elsewhere; I would rather be a doorkeeper in the house of my God than dwell in the tents of the wicked." Psalm 84:10

This scripture tells us that just one day in Heaven is better than one thousand days anywhere else. It says being a doorkeeper in God's house is better than living in the tents of the wicked.

In 2 Corinthians 5:1-2 Paul refers to the human body as a tent. *"For we know that if the tent that is our earthly home is destroyed, we have a building from God, a house not made with hands, eternal in the Heavens. For in this tent we groan, longing to put on our Heavenly dwelling..."*

While we live in our temporary tent we groan, longing for our eternal house. The very best of our lives here on earth, all of our highest highs, and all our most peaceful and joyous moments, are just a small preview of what God has prepared for us in Heaven. I don't think we will fully realize until we get there how unsatisfactory our lives were here. We think life in a tent is pretty good, but that's because we have not yet experienced life in God's mansion.

When my hopes and dreams are set on all this world has to offer, I grieve for all my son will miss out on by dying so young. It's hard to let go of the plans and expectations I had for my son's life here. But when I think of the perfection of Heaven and the unsurpassed blessing of living in God's presence, I have to stop feeling sad for all the days he missed out on here and instead rejoice for all the days he is spending in Heaven. It's not easy to make the transition from hoping in this life to hoping in what is to come. Meditating on Heaven helps me to get through the hard days of grief and set my sights on the indescribable joy of Heaven.

Prayer: Father God, thank you for the place you have prepared for us in Heaven and thank you for telling us about it so we won't get discouraged when life is disappointing. Thank you for the promise of thousands upon thousands of days living in Your courts. Help me to believe by faith that just one day in Heaven is better than a thousand days here on earth. Amen.

Replace Temporary Dreams With Eternal Dreams

'He will wipe every tear from their eyes. There will be no more death or mourning or crying or pain, for the old order of things has passed away. He who is seated on the throne said "I am making everything new!" Then he said, "Write this down, for these words are trustworthy and true"' Revelation 21:4-5

The earth as God originally created it was perfect. There were no death or mourning or crying or pain. Adam and Eve's sin brought a curse upon the earth and on all living things (Genesis 3). Sin entered the world and brought with it suffering, sorrow, despair and death. When Jesus died, He began the process of reversing sin's curse. We still suffer and die but suffering is redemptive and the dead in Christ are raised. When Jesus returns, He will complete the restoration by making all things new. When Jesus wipes away our tears in Heaven, nothing will ever hurt us again.

Death and mourning and crying and pain are the current order of things, but they are on their way out. One day they will pass away and become the old order of things. All wrongs will be made right.

In the above scripture, John is receiving a vision of Heaven. The One who is seated on the throne tells John, "Write this down, for these words are trustworthy and true."

The One seated on the throne is Jesus and we can trust in Him and His promises. We will be comforted. The former things will pass away. He will make everything new. He is trustworthy and true and so His words are trustworthy and true.

When my son died, many of my hopes and dreams died along with him. I am grieving the loss of my son and the dreams I had for him. I need to replace those lost dreams with new dreams. Better dreams. Heavenly and eternal dreams.

Prayer: Jesus, You are seated on the throne, trustworthy and true. I look forward to the day you will gently glide your hand across my cheek and wipe away, along with my tears, all my pain and sorrow forever. A day is coming when You will complete the restoration of the earth. I pray You will write these words on my heart and help me to replace my temporary dreams with eternal dreams. Amen.

Agree With Jesus

"*Father, I want those you have given me to be with me where I am, and to see my glory, the glory you have given me because you loved me before the creation of the world.*" *John 17:24*

In this prayer for all who would come to believe in Him, Jesus tells God it is His desire for those believers to be with Him in Heaven. In a sense, every time a believer dies, God is answering Jesus' prayer.

When we can agree with Jesus' prayer and tell God we would rather be in Heaven with Jesus than anywhere else, we can know we have made the transition from loving the world to loving the Lord first and best.

Some might say wanting to go to Heaven to escape the pain of the world, or wanting to go to Heaven to be reunited with a loved one is not the same thing as wanting to go to Heaven to be with Jesus. However, it's the world's disappointments and heartaches that open our eyes to the reality that this world is a broken and hurtful place and that what our hearts are really longing for is Jesus, who is in Heaven.

Pain removes our blinders so we can see clearly that there are suffering people all over the world. When we suffer we often gain compassion for other suffering people. When our focus is on eternity, we can easily forego worldly pursuits and gladly make personal sacrifices to help others.

The pain of grief is the blade that severed my affection for the world, but that doesn't make my longing for Heaven or my compassion for hurting people any less sincere.

Jesus wants us to be in Heaven with Him. Perhaps He longs for us as much as we long for Him. Perhaps He longs to return as much as we long for Him to return. When we pray ***"Your will be done on earth as it is in Heaven," (Matthew 6:10)*** we are praying for Jesus' return and are agreeing with Jesus in prayer.

Prayer: Jesus, thank You for praying for us to be with You and for making it clear that this world is not our home. I want to be with You where You are and to see Your glory! May Your will be done on earth as it is in Heaven. Amen.

Live as a Citizen of Heaven

"With the Lord a day is like a thousand years, and a thousand years are like a day. The Lord is not slow in keeping His promise, as some understand slowness. Instead He is patient with you, not wanting anyone to perish, but everyone to come to repentance. But the day of the Lord will come like a thief. The Heavens will disappear with a roar; the elements will be destroyed by fire, and the earth and everything in it will be laid bare. Since everything will be destroyed in this way, what kind of people ought you to be? You ought to live holy and godly lives as you look forward to the day of God and speed its coming." 2 Peter 3:11-12

This scripture refers to the day of Jesus' return. The apostle Peter is telling the early Christians, and us, that in light of Christ's return, we should live holy and godly lives, that we should look forward to His return, and somehow speed it's coming.

Peter says, because every man-made thing is marked for destruction, we should not live like the rest of the world lives. We should not work for earthly goods that will be destroyed. Since we are eternal beings and citizens of Heaven, we should act like it by living in a God-honoring way, always bearing in mind the certainty and imminence of Christ's return.

When Peter wrote this letter, he and other Christians were suffering persecution. Peter was encouraging the persecuted church to persevere in faith knowing that their suffering is temporary and Christ's return is certain.

In this letter, Peter explains that God is patiently waiting for more people to come to repentance, have faith in Jesus, and be saved for eternity. Peter seems to be saying that when we are suffering and we stand firm in our faith we are a living testimony to others of the hope we have in Christ. If we suffer well, perhaps more people will be saved and in that way we can speed Christ's return.

Prayer: Father God, thank You for the blood of Jesus that was shed for me so I could be counted as holy and godly. Help me to stand firm in my faith even when I suffer and to live my life as a citizen of Heaven. Amen.

Week Six

PERSEVERE

If I had to choose just one word to describe my son, Kyle, it would be perseverance. Kyle set high goals for himself and worked tirelessly to achieve them. He graduated from a private Christian high school with a 4.5 GPA and several AP classes under his belt. He got exceptionally high scores on all college entrance exams, and gained admission to UCLA, one of the most competitive universities in the country, and graduated with a degree in Economics.

When Kyle was in his junior year of high school he became interested in attending the U.S. Naval Academy. The application process was intense and extensive. Kyle interviewed for and gained a recommendation from a U.S. Senator, he was invited to spend a weekend at the Academy in Annapolis and was invited to several recruitment events. All this led him to believe he would be accepted into the academy. After the year-long process of applying, Kyle received the disappointing news that he was not accepted. Kyle believed it was due to his vision impairment. Kyle was offered a full ROTC scholarship, but he chose to decline it.

The determination and perseverance Kyle exhibited during the year-long application process were remarkably admirable. In order to make himself a more ideal candidate for the Naval Academy, Kyle joined his high school football team in his senior year even though he had never played football before. He worked exceedingly hard to get in top physical condition both for football and for the physical fitness test for the Academy. This was all added to his rigorous academic schedule.

I have never known anyone with more perseverance than my son Kyle. When the Bible tells us to persevere – to keep trying even when things are hard and are not working out for us – I think of Kyle. I do not share my son's drive for excellence or his attribute of perseverance. But giving up is certainly not what God wants from me, but rather for me to persevere in hope.

I sometimes think that after suffering such a devastating loss it would be understandable for me to just wait out the rest of my life on the sidelines until God brings me home. But that wouldn't bring God glory and it wouldn't honor my son's memory.

I am weak, but God is strong. I have no confidence in myself, but every confidence in God. By God's grace, the rest of my life will not be a slow death march but a steady stride toward the finish. And, like the apostle Paul, I want to be able to testify that I have been struck down, but not destroyed. (2 Cor. 4:9)

Run With Perseverance

"Therefore, since we are surrounded by such a great cloud of witnesses, let us throw off everything that hinders and the sin that so easily entangles. And let us run with perseverance the race marked out for us, fixing our eyes on Jesus, the pioneer and perfecter of faith. For the joy set before Him he endured the cross, scorning its shame, and sat down at the right hand of the throne of God. Consider Him who endured such opposition from sinners, so that you will not grow weary and lose heart."
Hebrews 12:1-3

The above scripture refers to the heroes of the faith mentioned in Hebrews 11. It tells us that because they are witnesses and they surround us, we should run with perseverance. This verse tells us there is a race that is marked out for us and the way to keep going is to keep our eyes on Jesus who established and will perfect our faith.

No one has a harder race marked out for them than Jesus had. He endured the cross for the joy that was to come. Like a race, the Christian life is about endurance and perseverance. Jesus was our forerunner and our example, but more than that, He has become our power and our assurance of victory. He has ascended to Heaven and is seated at the right hand of God where He intercedes for us. We keep our eyes on Christ to keep from growing weary and giving up. He is the joy that is set before us.

I often wonder if my son can see us from Heaven. I wonder if he knows what is going on here in the world and, more specifically, in the lives of his family and friends.

I want my son to be as proud of me as I have always been of him. When I think of my son sitting in the stadium with all the heroes of the faith, cheering me on, how can I not keep running?

Prayer: Father God, thank you for the certainty of knowing that I already have the victory in Christ, I just need to keep running for a little while longer. I pray you will give me supernatural endurance, let me hear the cheering of the crowd, and see Jesus and my loved ones waiting at the finish line. May I be empowered to do all things through Christ who gives me strength. Amen.

Pursue God

"The secret things belong to the Lord our God, but the things revealed belong to us and to our children forever, that we may follow all the words of this law." Deuteronomy 29:29

God has secrets. He hasn't told us everything. However, the things He has revealed to us belong to us and our children forever. God is covenantal and a promise-keeper. In the Bible He has made promises to all who will believe. All that He has promised to give us we will receive, although not necessarily when or how we expect it.

In Jeremiah 33:3 God said, *"Call to me and I will answer you and tell you great and unsearchable things you do not know."*

In the early days of my grief, I called on God constantly and He revealed things to me. Sometimes I shared them with others and sometimes I treasured them in my own heart.

Knowing that God's Word, the Holy Bible, is the main way God communicates with us in this age, I spent hours reading the Bible, looking for the answers and the assurances I needed. By His Holy Spirit, God would often illuminate a scripture and help me to know and understand it in a way I could not have apart from Him.

As I read through my Bible I came across many of God's promises that I had underlined, dated and written Kyle's name beside indicating that I had prayed that scripture for him. Even though I was confused about how God was going to keep all the promises He had previously given me for my son's life, I kept underlining new promises. Instead of believing that God did not and would not keep his promises, I believe that God will keep His promises in a different way, a different time, and a different place.

The above scriptures show that we can ask God our hard questions. We can ask Him to reveal His secrets to us and to tell us things we cannot otherwise know or understand. We can trust God to keep His promises to us and to our children.

Prayer: Father God, thank you that You desire to communicate with me and that it's okay to bring my hard questions to You and to seek knowledge from You. I pray that You will keep revealing Yourself to me so that I might trust You even more. It is in You that I live and move and have my being. (Acts 17:28) Amen.

Comfort Others

"Praise be to the God and Father of our Lord Jesus Christ, *the Father of compassion and the God of all comfort, who comforts us in all our troubles, so that we can comfort those in any trouble with the comfort we ourselves receive from God."*
2 Corinthians 1:3-4

This verse tells us that God is the Father of Jesus, the Father of compassion, and the God of all comfort. It tells us that God comforts us in all our troubles so that we can comfort others with the same comfort we receive from God. (God wants to make us into comforters.)

After my son died I wanted to talk to other parents who had lost children to learn how they survived it. I craved the understanding and compassion that only a fellow-sufferer could offer. I knew that only someone who had lost a child could possibly understand my pain. God brought several people who had lost children into my life who shared their stories and compassionately prayed for me. I am so grateful for each of them and the time they spent with me.

I also read many books written by parents who had lost children. In these two ways I received encouragement and felt a little less alone in my grief.

My first step out of isolation and back into the land of the living was to work at my friend's store. Even though I often cried while driving to and from the store, I was able to stay collected during business hours, to smile and interact with the customers and to pretend my life was normal. I never told anyone about my bereavement until one day a woman came in and told me that her daughter had recently died. I hugged her and told her about my son's death. We sat down right there in the store and shared our stories with each other. It helped. It all seemed like God's doing – getting me out of my house to help my grieving friend, then bringing me a new friend who was grieving like I was.

Prayer: God of all comfort, thank you for your plan to comfort us by bringing people into our lives who are able to show us compassion because they have been hurt in the same way. Help me to be a comforter to others. Amen.

Gain Strength From The Lord

"Even to your old age and gray hairs I am He, I am He who will sustain you. I have made you and I will carry you; I will sustain you and I will rescue you." Isaiah 46:4

The most important thing we need to know about God is that He is on our side. He is for us. He wants what is best for us. When we are suffering we have lots of questions that will probably not be answered to our satisfaction, but as long as we can be certain that God is with us and not against us, we can learn to live with the unanswered questions.

When we are suffering it often feels as though God has either turned against us or turned away from us in indifference. Neither will ever be true. When the worst happens and we are plunged into horrific suffering we rage at Heaven, "Where were you God?"

When we do this it shows we have mistaken God's promises. He promises to carry, sustain, and rescue us. If nothing ever happened that we were unable to handle on our own we wouldn't need His help. In a sense this is a promise that things will happen in our lives that we will not be able to handle.

God's help is available but we must be willing to accept it. Carrying, sustaining, and rescuing cannot be done with an unwilling participant. A person who is uncooperative and fighting against his rescuer cannot be carried, given sustenance, or rescued. The person has to either be willing to receive the offered help or be unconscious and unable to refuse.

In my grief I am at my weakest and I need God's power more than ever before. Paul writes, in *2 Corinthians 12:9, "...I will boast all the more gladly about my weaknesses, so that Christ's power may rest on me."* God's power is made perfect in us when we are weak. We are actually the strongest we can ever be when we are at our weakest because that is when we are willing to accept God's help and His power can work in us and through us.

Prayer: Lord God, I need Christ's power to rest on me. Please make me willing to be carried, sustained, and rescued by You. I want and need your help. Thank you that your promise is for a life time. Even to my old age and gray hairs. Amen.

Work for the Lord

"Whatever you do, work at it with all your heart, as working for the Lord, not for men, since you know that you will receive an inheritance from the Lord as a reward. It is the Lord Christ you are serving." Colossians 3:23-24

This scripture tells us to do all our work as though we are doing it for the Lord, because we are. Some Bible versions say "whatever your hands find to do."

Working with all our heart, as to the Lord, means giving it our all, doing our best, aiming at excellence in all we do. And it says we are to do this in "whatever we do." Not just church work or Christian service but whatever we do – playing, working, studying, housework, yardwork, relationships, worship...whatever.

When my son was in middle school our pastor taught about spiritual fasting, saying that when we fast we shouldn't tell anyone but should keep it a secret between us and God. The day after hearing the sermon, my husband took our sons to play golf. When he bought lunch for himself and the boys, Kyle did not want to eat and would not say why. My husband soon figured out that Kyle was already obediently fasting and keeping it a secret.

My son had this quality of whole-heartedness. He was so diligent, competent, and driven to excel. He liked to do everything to the best of his ability and it hurt him deeply when he felt as though he had failed or fallen short. He set high goals for himself and almost always achieved them. It was heart-breaking for him to fail because he put his whole heart into all that he did.

This scripture doesn't say God is pleased when we succeed, but rather that He is pleased when we work with our whole heart. God isn't looking for results, He's looking for obedient and devout hearts.

1 Samuel 16:7 says, "...*for God sees not as man sees, for man looks at the outward appearance, but the LORD looks at the heart.*"

Prayer: Father God, thank you that you see our hearts and thank you that my loved one's heart was pleasing to you in so many ways. I pray You will supply me with motivation to work with excellence for you in whatever my hands find to do. Help me to care more about having a right heart attitude than achieving results. Amen.

Remember Life is Short

"Show me, Lord, my life's end and the number of my days; let me know how fleeting my life is. You have made my days a mere handbreadth; the span of my years is as nothing before you. Everyone is but a breath, even those who seem secure."
Psalm 39:4-5

This scripture says that life is fleeting, a "mere handbredth", and "but a breath." In the scope of eternity, there doesn't seem to be much difference between dying as an infant and living to be a Centenarian. Either way, life is brief. Experiencing the sudden and unexpected death of a loved one makes one mindful of the brevity of life.

In 1 Corinthians 15, the apostle Paul is teaching about the resurrection of the dead. In verse 19 he states, *"If only for this life we have hope in Christ, we are of all people most to be pitied."* And then in verse 32, *"If the dead are not raised, let us eat and drink, for tomorrow we die."* I believe Paul is saying that if there were no eternal life then this temporary life is meaningless. It is the hope of eternal life in Heaven that gives our lives meaning and purpose.

It is because we have the assurance of Heaven that we are able to endure all the heartbreak of this fallen world. It is because we know we will spend eternity in Heaven that we can let go of selfish desires and be freed to love God and other people. We don't need to have the worldly mindset of taking in all we can before we die. We don't need "bucket lists" of things we want to see and do before we die. Death from this life will be our birth into Heaven and we will have all of eternity to see and do exciting and wonderful things.

When life is good we want it to go on forever, but when we are suffering we long for Heaven. No matter what our perception is of the passing of time, in the end we will know our stay on earth has been brief. If we have lived our short life with eternity in mind it has not been meaningless.

Prayer: Father God, thank you for the promise that the best is yet to come. Please help me to live a meaningful life, yet keep me from getting too caught up in the day-to-day grind. Help me to keep my eyes fixed on my real home in Heaven. Amen.

Anticipate Immortality

"'Listen, I tell you a mystery: We will not all sleep, but we will all be changed – in a flash, in the twinkling of an eye, at the last trumpet. For the trumpet will sound, the dead will be raised imperishable, and we will be changed. For the perishable must clothe itself with the imperishable, and the mortal with immortality." 1 Corinthians 15:51-53*

In the apostle Paul's letter to the Corinthians he says that not everyone will die before Jesus' return and the resurrection of the dead, but all will be changed. All will be given new bodies that are imperishable, indestructible, and have new abilities.

We have all been living under a death sentence from the moment we were born. Our bodies are quickly aging and moving toward death. What will it be like to have a body that will never age and never be sick or injured? As an aging recreational runner, I imagine one of the best things about living in a perfect body in Heaven will be having the ability to run without growing tired and never being hindered by dwindling knee cartilage or other bodily afflictions.

When Jesus appeared in His resurrection body he was able to appear and disappear from rooms and yet his disciples were able to touch Him.

Perhaps the bodies we will be given at the resurrection will be like Christ's body after His resurrection.

1 John 3:2 says, *"...now we are children of God, and what we will be has not yet been made known. But we know that when Christ appears, we shall be like him, for we shall see him as he is."*

In addition to having perfect and immortal bodies, we will be morally perfect – unable to sin. I don't think we can fully fathom what that will be like. No more sinful thoughts to battle and no more struggles with self-control. No feelings of inadequacy, regret, guilt, or remorse. All peace, all joy, all love, all the time.

Prayer: Father God, thank you for your promise that the dead will be raised imperishable and immortal. I long to have a perfect immortal body and perfect moral character. I long for an end to all death, mourning, crying and pain. I long to live with You forever. Please come soon, Lord Jesus. Amen.

HAVE CONFIDENT FAITH

It was February 13, 2014, two years since my son, Kyle, was taken to Heaven. That morning, I once again handed God all the pieces of my broken heart. In my morning prayer I asked God to show me, somehow, sometime that day that He is still in control and that He loves and cares for my family and I.

My husband and I were in Florida for two weeks, taking a break from the harsh winter we were having in Missouri and we had no real plans for the day. We thought we might go kayaking and look for manatees, go for a hike, or do something else outdoors. After several false starts, wrong turns, and foiled plans, we ended up right where God wanted us to be – on St. Pete Beach after a storm. It was cold and windy by Florida standards, but since we had lived on the northern California coast for most of our lives it felt about right to us and we mostly had the beach to ourselves.

We had been on this beach just a few days before but it looked very different that day. The storm had dredged up and washed ashore a variety of sea debris – shells, driftwood, and seaweed. I began noticing some large mollusks, lots of them, everywhere. I stopped to inspect one and saw that it looked just like a Valentine heart folded in half. I nudged it a little with my foot, apprehensive about what might be living inside, then asked my husband to open it. When it was opened it only had a little wet sand inside and it looked like a perfect Valentine heart. As soon as it was spread open I knew in my spirit this was it – this was God answering my prayer and showing me His love. This was my valentine from the Lord and His assurance to me that He is still in control, that Kyle is with Him, well-loved and well-cared for, and He will continue to be faithful and loving to my family and I.

I had the idea to make a heart in the sand out of some of the shell hearts and write Kyle's name inside. It was not hard to find enough shells – they were strewn everywhere. It was thrilling running up and down the beach collecting the shells, each one a love letter from my Heavenly Father. After we finished making the large heart, we outlined Kyle's name with smaller shells. We worked on this for a while, collecting shells then kneeling into the sand to put them in place. When we finished, we stood and admired our work, then took a walk a little further down the beach. When we turned around and began walking back toward our "love monument" we saw something we had not noticed before. About 100 feet inland was a flagpole with an American flag whipping wildly in the wind. It was directly in line with our monument. Our son was a true patriot, so much so that when we built a memorial garden in our yard at home we centered it around a tall flag pole that displays the American flag. We had not seen the flag and had chosen the spot to place our shells at random. On that entire miles-long beach we could not have placed our monument in a more appropriate place!

The valentine shells would have been enough, but God wanted to be sure we understood this was for us. This was no coincidence – this was the God of the universe reaching down from Heaven to communicate to us what we really needed to know that day. He is there. He is here. He knows and He cares.

Have Confident Faith

"Now faith is confidence in what we hope for and assurance about what we do not see." Hebrews 11:1

This scripture is about faith in God's promises. Heaven is a promise from God. We hope for Heaven, but we do not yet see it. God wants us to have confidence in our hope for Heaven and to be assured that it is real.

Because my son lives there, I have strived to learn all I can know about Heaven, both the current Heaven and the Heaven that is to come. I have always believed Heaven is real and unfathomably good, but what I have recently learned is how much like earth Heaven will be when all scriptures are ultimately fulfilled and Heaven comes down to earth.

The Bible doesn't tell us a lot about the current Heaven, but we know it is amazing because Jesus called it Paradise. (Luke 23:43) The current Heaven is described briefly in at least two places in the Bible.

In Acts 7:54-60, Stephen, who was martyred by being stoned to death for his faith, saw Heaven and Jesus at the moment of his death. Stephen proclaims, *"Behold, I see the Heavens opened and the Son of Man standing at the right hand of God." (Acts 7:56)*

In Luke 16:19-31, Lazarus, who had a hard life, is now being comforted in Heaven. *"The poor man died and was carried by the angels to Abraham's side." (Luke 16:22)*

There is a lot more that can be surmised about the current Heaven from scripture. Randy Alcorn has researched and written extensively about Heaven, both the current Heaven and the Heaven that is to come, and I highly recommend his books.

While I don't know everything about the current Heaven, I know from scripture that Jesus lives there and it is a place of comfort. And now, my son lives there too. I am so convinced of the surety and magnificence of Heaven that I am anxious to go there.

Prayer: Father God, thank you for the promise of Heaven and the gift of faith which only comes from You. Thank you for opening my spiritual eyes so that I might be convinced of what my physical eyes have yet to see. Please build up my confidence by increasing my faith. Amen.

Believe God's Promises

"All these people were still living by faith when they died. They did not receive the things promised; they only saw them and welcomed them from a distance, admitting that they were foreigners and strangers on earth. People who say such things show that they are looking for a country of their own. If they had been thinking of the country they had left, they would have had opportunity to return. Instead, they were longing for a better country – a Heavenly one. Therefore God is not ashamed to be called their God, for he has prepared a city for them." Hebrews 11:13-16

"These people" are all the heroes of faith in the Old Testament. This scripture tells us they were still living by faith when they died. They had not received the things God had promised them. This was important for me to see because God had not yet fulfilled all His promises for my son's life. I needed to understand that it was not over and there was still plenty of time and plenty of ways for God to fulfill His promises.

God knit my son together in such a wonderful way and gave him such remarkable qualities. I always expected big things from my son and knew God would use him and all his abilities in spectacular ways. When he died I wondered, who would now do all the things my son would have done if he had lived a full life? I have come to understand my son did live a full life – it was the amount of time God gave him here on earth. (Psalm 139:16, Job 14:5)

My son's transition from this life into his life in Heaven does not mean he will not still do great things and will not reach his potential. He will! God had much bigger plans for my son than either I or my son had. God's plans are eternal.

The above scripture describes people of faith as foreigners and strangers here on earth and says they are looking for a better country. As Christians, we are residents of Heaven and are foreigners and strangers here on earth. We should be longing for a better, Heavenly country.

Prayer: Father God, thank You for keeping me from being too comfortable and at home in this world. I am longing for a better country – a Heavenly country. Help me to believe Your promises. I pray You will never be ashamed to be called my God. Amen.

Hold on to Your Confidence

"So do not throw away your confidence; it will be richly rewarded. You need to persevere so that when you have done the will of God, you will receive what he has promised. For, 'In just a little while, he who is coming will come and will not delay.' And, 'But my righteous one shall live by faith. And I take no pleasure in the one who shrinks back.'" Hebrews 10:35-38

This scripture encourages us to hold onto our confidence in God and His promises. It assures us that we will receive what God has promised, but we must persevere and do His will because Jesus is coming soon. He may show up at any moment and we don't want Him to find us shrinking back, but boldly and courageously holding onto our faith.

I admit my faith took a big hit when my son died. I lost confidence. I didn't throw it away, it was torn from me. Why would God do this to my son, to me, and to our family? Why did my son have to die? Why was this great loss and sadness brought upon my family?

Even with all my unanswered questions, I still loved and trusted God. I knew He was my only hope. I needed to know He was still going to fulfill all His promises. This scripture tells me that He will.

While initially I did seem to waiver in my faith, my faith has actually grown stronger and more sincere because it is no longer dependent on God performing for me by answering my prayers the way I expect and keeping my life trouble-free and pain-free. My faith is not in having perfect circumstances and a perfect life. My faith is in God's perfect character, perfect love, and perfect faithfulness.

I can experience the joy of The Lord in any and all circumstances. I can have joy in my sorrow, and hope in my despair.

"I can do all things through Christ who strengthens me." (Phil. 4:8)

Prayer: Father God, I pray You will keep me strong and that you will not only keep me from shrinking back but will move me forward. When my heart hurts thinking of the good things I have lost, help me to think instead of all the good things that are still to come because Jesus is coming soon. Keep me confident in You – my Savior, my Redeemer, my Lord. Amen.

Be Assured of God's Presence

"Fear not, for I have redeemed you; I have summoned you by name; you are mine. When you pass through the waters, I will be with you; and when you pass through the rivers, they will not sweep over you. When you walk through the fire, you will not be burned; the flames will not set you ablaze." **Isaiah 43:1-2**

In this scripture, God speaks through the prophet Isaiah to tell the Israelites (and us) not to be afraid because we belong to Him. He promises to be with us as we face all manner of dangerous situations – waters and rivers that threaten to sweep us away and flames of perilous fire through which we must walk. God does not promise to keep us from facing these dangerous situations, but to deliver us through them by walking with us to ensure that we are not swept away or set ablaze. He doesn't say we won't get wet or feel the heat.

In his book, <u>A Grief Observed</u>, C.S. Lewis said, "No one ever told me that grief felt so like fear."

I agree with Lewis that often grief does feel a lot like fear, both emotionally and physically. Emotionally there is the feeling of vulnerability – that you have lost control and are at the mercy of others. Now that this terrible thing has happened, any other random terrible thing can happen too. The world becomes a very unsafe place. Physically, there is a racing heart to match racing thoughts, like the adrenaline jolt of a fight-or-flight situation that never relents.

God doesn't say we won't suffer. He says when we suffer we will not be alone and it will not be the end of us.

In the hymn, How Firm a Foundation, a fiery furnace is said to serve the purpose of consuming our dross so that we shine like gold.

"When through fiery trials thy pathways shall lie,
My grace, all sufficient, shall be thy supply;
The flame shall not hurt thee; I only design
Thy dross to consume, and thy gold to refine."

Prayer: Father God, I would never choose the hard path of suffering for myself, however, I do want to shine like gold and I do have a lot of dross. Please reassure me daily of your promise to be with me and to carry me through the fire and water. Amen.

Be Confident in God's Restoration Power

"Lift up your eyes and look around; all your sons gather and come to you. As surely as I live, declares the lord, you will wear them all as ornaments; you will put them on, like a bride."
Isaiah 49:18

My bible notes tell me this scripture is about God's promise for the restoration of Israel and that ornaments symbolize strength and joy. Some of the commentary I read on this verse also indicates that in addition to promising the restoration of Israel, it is a foreshadowing of salvation through Jesus Christ and a promise of a Heavenly reunion.

I have this scripture underlined in my Bible with *"3/2/08 Bible study retreat"* written in the margin next to it. On the last day of the retreat I was attending, we were given sections of scripture to read and reflect upon. This scripture stood out to me because it speaks of restoration and of sons. I am the mother of three sons and in March of 2008 I was feeling quite melancholy about being on the verge of becoming an empty-nester.

My two oldest sons were already away at college, one several hours to the north and one several hours to the south. My youngest son was finishing up his senior year of high school with plans to leave for college in the fall. This verse gave me hope that one day there would be restoration for my family. We would be scattered all over the state of California, but one day we would all be together again.

I had no idea at the time that just a few weeks later my husband would bring me the news that his job was being relocated from California to Arkansas and we would be leaving at the end of the year. Restoration of our family now seemed unlikely to happen anytime soon since my husband and I would be moving and leaving our sons behind. How and when was God going to bring our family back together?

When my son died I realized our family reunion will not happen on this side of Heaven. On that day I will put on strength and joy as a bride. It will happen, as surely as God lives.

Prayer: Father God, help me to be confident that a day is coming when you will restore our family. May I look forward to that day knowing it will happen as surely as You live. Please keep me optimistic about the future. Amen

Trust God to Hold You

"But Jacob replied, "I will not let you go unless you bless me." Genesis 32:26

Like Jacob, I wrestled with God. (Genesis 32) Unlike Jacob, I did not stubbornly hold on for a blessing. God let my son die and left me here to live through it. Like so many other suffering people I wanted to know why, if God is able to do all things and He loves us, does he allow us to be hurt so deeply?

This was the question that was on my mind ten months after my son died as I walked for miles and miles on a California beach. I wanted desperately to understand why God let my son die. We needed him in our family. We could not spare him. Why God? Why?

I stopped and sat on a large piece of driftwood and looked out at the ocean. I wondered how it would feel to walk out into the water, past the breaking waves, and keep going. What would it be like to fall asleep twirling around in the cold salty water and then to wake up in Heaven? My despair was really deep that day. I was missing my son and feeling hopeless that I would ever feel whole again. I cried out to God and told Him I just didn't have it in me to keep going. In my spirit and in my mind I heard God telling me it was okay if I couldn't hold on to Him because he was holding on to me.

Like a drowning person who cannot be helped as long as they are thrashing and struggling, I had to stop resisting and let God save me. Knowledge of God's reasons for allowing my son to die will not help heal my broken heart and there is no explanation that will ever be good enough for me. If answering my questions would have helped me on that day, I believe God would have revealed the answers to me. There was nothing better He could do for me than to promise to hold on to me when I could no longer find the strength to hold on to Him.

Only the unending, supernatural love and care of the All-Mighty Sovereign of the universe can give me the strength I need to keep showing up for my life every day. On my good days I am holding on to God; on all my days God is holding on to me.

Prayer: Father God, help me to feel secure knowing You never let go of my son and You will never let go of me. Your love and care for us will always be enough. Amen.

Ask God for a New Heart

"And I will give you a new heart, and a new spirit I will put within you. And I will remove the heart of stone from your flesh and give you a heart of flesh." Ezekiel 36:26

In this scripture, God was talking to the Israelites and telling them what He would do for them when they came back to Him. When we close our heart to God it becomes like stone – cold, hard and dead. But when we return to God He removes our stone-like heart and give us a new heart of flesh along with a new spirit.

The overwhelming pain of my loss and my grief closed and hardened my heart. It just hurt so much. Since I could not accept that God had allowed my son to die, neither could I accept the comfort and strength God wanted to give me.

I knew and trusted God as the sovereign Creator and Sustainer of the universe. I knew Him to be good, kind, and merciful. I knew he chose my son from before the beginning of time to belong to Him and that He had good plans for my son's life. What I could not fathom was how, with everything I knew, God could allow my son to die.

Even though I did not want to believe that God would ever allow such pain into our lives, what I wanted to believe even less was that God had nothing to do with it – that He either didn't care or wasn't in control. The Bible is filled with evidence of God's love for His people and His power over all creation. What I had to reconcile was that God never lost control and was never uninformed about my son's condition. God chose to bring my son to Heaven.

I need to learn to humbly accept that everything that happens in my life comes from God's hand. I already know how to trust God when life is good, what I need to learn is how to keep trusting Him when He allows my loved ones and I to suffer.

Prayer: Father God, I acknowledge You as the Sovereign Creator and Sustainer of the universe. Not a bird falls from the sky apart from You knowing it. Nothing is out of your reach or control. Please remove my heart of stone and begin the flow of your life-giving blood back into my heart again. Amen.

CONCLUSION

It's May 28, 2015 and it's Kyle's 28TH birthday. I'm sitting where no mother wants to sit – at my son's gravestone. I've brought fresh flowers, a beach chair, and a coffee drink. I plan to stay awhile. I sit in the sunshine and think about my son. I think about his life. I think about his death.

Oh God, why does it have to be this way?

Oh Kyle, I miss you so much!

Grief is often called a journey and, for me, it's a journey that will not end until I see my son again. But I have come a long way. My expression of grief has become more of a sad, resigned sigh rather than an ear-piercing, guttural wail or a foot-stomping, fist-shaking tantrum. I have accepted what has happened. Not accepted in the sense that it's okay with me, but in the sense that I know I can't do anything to change it.

There have been days on this journey when I have felt completely alone, but I know I never have been. God has been faithful to stick with me even when I have been utterly unfaithful to Him.

In the Bible, in 1 Samuel 7:3-15, Samuel sets a stone as a monument to acknowledge the Lord's faithfulness to the Israelites.

"Then Samuel took a stone and set it up between Mizpah and Shen and called its name Ebenezer; for he said, "Till now the Lord has helped us.""1 Samuel 7:12

This stone-setting is done throughout the Old Testament by sojourners who have experienced God's power and faithfulness.

This grief journey I am on is a dirty, sweaty climb up a steep and treacherous mountain. I fall, slip and lose ground. I'm tired, bruised and broken, but I'm compelled to press on. There's a fog eclipsing the summit. How much further? What lies ahead?

I pause on the rocky path and turn slowly to look back down the mountain. I've come further than I thought. It's been impossibly difficult, beyond my ability, but somehow I have been able. I see the people who have helped me and encouraged me along the way and I know it was God who put them in place.

I'm walking a path that no person wants to walk. I am doing this hard thing that I don't have the strength to do.

"Till now the Lord has helped me."

And He will not stop helping me. He will not leave me alone.

Jesus is not waiting at the top but has come all the way down to bring me all the way up.

I lay down the weighty heart-shaped stone I've been carrying – the stone with the word "Inconsolable." I turn the stone over and I write a new word. I write The Word. I write JESUS.

I turn from the darkness and into the light and I set a monument to God's faithfulness.

On my son's gravestone is a picture of him taken at his college graduation. He is smiling big and beautiful – the whole world ahead of him. I think of Kyle celebrating his birthday in Heaven today and I know he is smiling big and beautiful – all of eternity ahead of him.

I sip my coffee and turn my face into the warm sun that wraps around me and holds me like a hug from Heaven.

"...ye cannot in your present state understand eternity...That is what mortals misunderstand. They say of some temporal suffering, "No future bliss can make up for it," not knowing that Heaven, once attained, will work backwards and turn even that agony into a glory."
-CS Lewis, The Great Divorce

ABOUT THE AUTHOR

Julie Jones is married and the mother of three amazing young men. Two are living here on earth, and one is living in Heaven.

Jones has a degree in Early Childhood Education and has previously worked as a preschool teacher and a newspaper reporter, along with a variety of other jobs.

Jones has served as a leader in Bible Study Fellowship and as a Mini-Missionary with The Rafiki Foundation.

Jones has lived most of her life in Northern California and currently resides in southwest Missouri.

You may contact the author at set.on.things.above@gmail.com

You may follow the author's volunteer work with the Rafiki Foundation on her face book page.
www.facebook.com/Myminimission

All profits from the sale of this book will be used to purchase library books for The Rafiki Foundation.

Recommended Reading:

Heaven, by Randy Alcorn
We Shall See God, by Randy Alcorn
Seeing the Unseen, by Randy Alcorn
Eternal Perspectives, by Randy Alcorn
If God is Good, by Randy Alcorn
hand in Hand, by Randy Alcorn
A Grief Observed, by C.S. Lewis
Heaven, Your Real Home, by Joni Earekson Tada
When God Weeps, by Joni Earekson Tada
A Place of Healing, by Joni Earekson Tada
The Heaven Answer Book, by Billy Graham
Lament For A Son, by Nicholas Wolterstorff
Heaven, My Father's House, by Anne Graham Lotz
Why?, by Anne Graham Lotz
A Path Through Suffering, by Elisabeth Elliott
Holding On To Hope, by Nancy Guthrie
Be Still, My Soul, by Nancy Guthrie
O Love That Will Not Let Me Go, by Nancy Guthrie
Choosing To See, by Mary Beth Chapman
A Grace Disguised, by Jerry Sittser
Walking with God through Pain and Suffering, by Timothy Keller
Man's Search for Meaning, by Viktor E. Frankl
Appointments with Heaven, by Reggie Anderson
Suffering and the Sovereignty of God, by John Piper
When Heaven Is Silent, by Ronn Dunn
A Severe Mercy, by Sheldon Vanauken
Treasures in Darkness, by Sharon Betters
Amish Grace, by Donald B. Kraybill and others